Management

A different perspective

Andrew W. Jones

Copyright © 2013 by Andrew W. Jones

ISBN-13: 978-1494771720
ISBN-10: 1494771721

All Rights Reserved. No part of this book may be used or reproduced in any manner without written permission of the author, except in the case of brief quotations in articles and/or reviews.

For information contact the author at **author@andrewjonesbooks.com** or by visiting the author's website at **www.andrewjonesbooks.com**

Printed in the United States of America

10 9 8 7 6 5 4 3 2 1

"Talent hits a target no one else can hit; genius hits a target no one else can see."

Arthur Schopenhauer

Introduction

This book is a compilation of some of my college papers. It is a collection of ideas with research references to help new managers have a different perspective on ways of doing business. It is also an analysis of management methods that the employee may want to think about in order to predict certain behaviors and process methods they may experience in the workplace. This is not a how-to book, rather a why-are-you-doing-that book. What is our purpose? Is it a drive or motivation that we have inside us that constantly seeks a new avenue of approach to resolving conflicts in our current situation? It may be a reflection of our greed and actions that are required to achieve that which we desire but are slightly ill-equipped to accomplish without such a motivational factor.

We should periodically ask ourselves what drives our motivations; especially if we are managers. Motivations such as going to work and going to church may be slightly different. Our motivation to want to be home on the weekend may not be a desire to spend time with our family; it may be a desire to lounge in front of a television. An intended purpose can drive us to the breaking point. If we set our goals too high, we will never achieve them and we will be depressed and eat too much ice cream. How much is too much ice cream? Well, I suppose we could say that we are depressed if we sit around and eat a gallon of it in one sitting due to the stress we are feeling in our lives. To get back on track, we should do a self-assessment to see what motivates us from time-to-time. I am motivated by my family, my need to succeed and of course, money. I would not work so hard for free, and I doubt anyone else would either. I told that to a manager once. He made the statement that if you are just here for the money, you need to find another place of employment. Well, why else would we be here? I told him that the day he stopped paying me is the day I walked off the job. I have a family support. Of course that is my own opinion, but I just know that everyone I worked for felt the same way. If you want proof of that, stop paying your employees and see how many stay around the coffee pot.

Table of Contents

Chapter	Title
Chapter 1	Business Challenges
Chapter 2	B2B Messages
Chapter 3	Strategies
Chapter 4	Professional Values and Ethics
Chapter 5	Professional Workplace Dilemma
Chapter 6	Past, Present, and Future
Chapter 7	Organizational Philosophies and Technology
Chapter 8	Function of Management
Chapter 9	Management Planning
Chapter 10	Management and Leadership
Chapter 11	Critical Thinking Application
Chapter 12	System of Inquiry
Chapter 13	Mind and Consciousness of Machines and Humans
Chapter 14	Metaphor/Humanity
Chapter 15	Critical Thinking and Society

Chapter 16   Solve a Problem
Chapter 17   Individual Strengths and
             Problem Solving Techniques

Chapter 18   Value of Technology

References

Chapter 1   Business Challenges

Depending on your target market, YouTube can be an asset to small business in that the majority of users are between 12 and 17 years of age. This age group probably still relies on their parents for a source of disposable income, so if businesses can deliver a product that is craved by these teenagers (electronics, cool clothes, new ideas), they could run an advertisement to a huge audience at a low cost. As a television or film executive, I would target that audience with film trailers of up and coming movies, to include independent films that are relevant to that age group. The text mentions the possibility of copyright infringement by persons who upload bootlegged films, but most movie producers allow a portion of this to happen for greater exposure of their products. As a film executive, I would invest in YouTube's antipiracy software just to level the playing field. I would suggest that new movie clips be limited to a couple minutes of action, just to entice the audience, but not to give away any good scenes (Turban, King, McKay, Marshall, Lee & Viehland, 2008).

According to one analyst, "[The business of] Attracting and retaining loyal customers remains the most important issue for any selling company, including e-tailers" (Turban, King, McKay, Marshall, Lee & Viehland, 2008, p. 167). Increased information flow can undermine the success of established brands because consumers can go online and research data pertaining to a particular product, or have instant access to that company's competitors. Word-of-mouth and varying opinions can spread quickly on the internet, building up the reputation of a new product or brand, or destroying it overnight.

Manufacturers and online business owners can combat the effects of this hyper-competiveness by providing the best customer service and interacting directly with the customer to regain or build brand loyalty. Technologies such as improved search engines and social networking sites make it impossible for online companies to ignore the potential impact of an unsatisfied customer (Turban, et al, 2008). Organizational objectives include building consumer trust in companies and products. Consumer behavior involves a multi-step process including research, attitudes, and underlying reasons for product purchase. Consumers learn to trust companies, analyze the risk involved with purchasing (online through electronic means), and the intention or willingness to buy from a certain retailer or e-tailer (DMSRetail Inc., 2010).

Consumer Trust

Consumer trust affects the online marketplace. The online marketplace will not survive without a way to protect consumers from fraud and abuse. Typically, an online consumer will have more trust in a larger organization or business with an established presence and effective track-record. Consumers are more likely to gain trust in online stores that also have a physical location. Reasons for this include the businesses stake in protecting existing reputation and stock assets. Online consumers expect privacy and collection of personal data to be a top priority (DMSRetail Inc., 2010). Consumer feedback forms, warranties, guarantees, and customer service response documents can build consumer trust. These items enable e-commerce by allowing customers to interact with business owners. In a typical brick-and-mortar store, a customer can easily walk into the customer service department and speak with a manager. In an online environment, the owner or manager could be several thousand miles away. Consumers must also trust the device (computer) they are using to make purchases. Anti-virus software provides a high degree of protection to online e-shoppers. Firewall software also can be used. Consumer risk in the online business environment can also affect purchasing power and business profits. Risk is how dangerous an individual consumer believes a purchase to be. In the electronic commerce (EC) environment, models of consumer behavior are helpful in determining the underlying causes of consumer apprehension or execution of a purchase. Variables affecting consumers include "independent variables, intervening or moderating variables, the decision-making process, and dependent variables" (Turban, King, McKay, Marshall, Lee, & Viehland, 2008, p. 157). Risk enables e-commerce by causing a questioning attitude and allowing competition to drive prices lower. Too much risk can avert a potential customer. Risk also opens the door for consumer protection software and companies like Vericheck. Risk will be a deterrent for some consumers and will cause them to make purchases at traditional stores exclusively. Consumers want to know that they can securely deliver data to its intended recipient; not a hacker or identity thief. E-loyalty is a term that refers to the consumer's potential of returning to a certain business for more products after a satisfactory experience. "Customer acquisition and retention is a critical success factor in e-tailing" (Turban, King, McKay, Marshall, Lee, & Viehland, 2008, p. 167). The Internet provides a way for customers to conduct e-business and prepares the consumer for risks involved with purchases. Gimmicks are a way of attracting new customers and adequate customer service is a way to attract existing customers. Customer service is vital in online commerce. Competition is fierce and customers have many choices in EC. E-loyalty enables online commerce by allowing businesses to project future sales and growth. A recent survey revealed that "convenience, web store environment, and online shopping enjoyment" contributed directly to the consumer buying experience (Prasad & Aryasri, 2009, p. 73). A simple can attract consumer loyalty. Market and motivation research are two ways to determine why consumers buy certain products (Pickle, Hal, Abrahamson & Royce, 1983).

Sample Persuasive Message

Man may think material wealth into existence! Someone could read a mind! I had my own psychic experience several years ago. I wrote a story about a man by a certain name. A woman who I worked with said she received a phone call from the FBI and the woman who called (from the FBI office) asked her if she knew a man by a certain name. At work, she casually told me about her story, and I just about fell out of my chair. She had no prior knowledge of my short story. After many months of pondering on this matter, I began to question certain aspects of this situation. It could have been mere coincidence that the man in question shared the same name as the man in my fictional story.

I have tried to figure out how my coworker could have arrived at the same name for the man in my story. "Why would the FBI call and ask for this man, leave little details about the reasoning for their questioning, and call a known friend?" I have since erased the story from my computer because at first, I will admit I was taken by surprise in a most uncomfortable way. Tonight, I will set all fears aside and venture out into the summer air.

The stage is set. The house lights dim down for the anticipation of tonight's performance. The club is full of people talking and dancing, drinking, and flirting. Someone takes the stage; another grand performance from one of the best known psychics in Texas. "What a crowd and what a wonderful experience!" Join in tonight for a mystical evening with South Texas Legend, C. Alto Clearly.

Analysis

"The term "hook" comes from the advertising and public relations fields, in which presenters have only a few seconds to make a point" (Roebuck & McKenney, 2006, p. 102). The sample persuasive message is an attempt to draw a crowd for a performing psychic. The message starts off with a couple of wild claims. I am the sender and my intended audience is from all walks of life. I want to appear credible to the audience. The message has an ambiguous but exciting tone intended to hook the audience as potential customers. I am targeting the listener's interest, desire, and emotional appeal (Roebuck & McKenney, 2006). The receiver is whoever hears this add on the radio or reads it in the newspaper. I used sensationalism to create an expected visual experience. I also included a personal experience to "set-the-stage" for the event. In summary, persuasive tactics are used online and in direct markets. Technology has increased business in EC because of instant feedback, committed customer service capabilities, and easy transactions. Security will always be a risk when a transaction is made via electronic devices. Customer loyalty toward brands and companies continues to be steady in the online environment. Out sourcing of customer service departments can lead to a lack of consumer loyally; consumers perceive more risk. Trust takes time to build. Word-of-mouth is still an effective means for businesses to prove they are reliable and trustworthy to online consumers. Retailers must take this into consideration when persuading customers to purchase products. The role of the retailer, a sales intermediary, is to operate between the customer and the organization which makes the good or provides the service. Prior to the internet, retailing was accomplished in "brick-and-mortar" facilities, called stores. Now, a new generation of retailers can be found online, referred to as "e-tailers." They conduct e-commerce by means of technology on the World Wide Web (Turban, King, McKay, Marshall, Lee & Viehland, 2008). A few examples of these are amazon.com, e-bay, and barnesandnoble.com.

New terms like electronic retailing and e-tailing models have been added to a growing vocabulary in the online business community. New concepts like, electronic real estate market, and online trading of stocks and bonds have placed competition in the age old way of doing business, allowing more people to have greater access to the way their money is invested and spent (Turban, et al, 2008). We also learned that a consumer behavior model consists of Independent (or uncontrollable) variables, Intervening (or moderating) variables, the decision-making process, and the dependent variables (Turban, et al, 2008, p. 157). "Customers can switch loyalty online easily and quickly. Therefore, enhancing e-loyalty (e.g., through e-loyalty programs) is a must" (Turban, et al, 2008, p. 208). This is where the role of the "intelligence agent" is important, in that they collect and interpret information and trends about how and why consumers behave in certain ways (Turban, et al, 2008). These are conducted through mystery shoppers and consumer surveys.

Business Communication Skills are important in regards to electronic and business correspondence. It explains the proper organization of business writing. Also covered in the chapter is the correct and incorrect way of handling the delivery of bad news, and saying "no" in the business world (Roebuck & McKenney, 2006).

Chapter 2 B2B Messages

Business communication over the Internet is a normal mode of operation for large and small businesses. Personal interaction is lacking in some online business operations, but tools like Facebook can build team bonding and strengthen business ties and communication. Other unique business tools include e-mail, cell phones, and electronically sent interoffice memorandums (Christensen, 2010). Technology has increased business to businesses effectiveness. According to Business Communications Group, (2010), "Search engine optimization (SEO), or organic search marketing, is an integral part of any b2b internet marketing strategy," (para. 1).

Business to business communication is vital to the success of any organization. New technologies allow businesses to interact with each other with minimal loss of time. Effective communication involves many steps to be effective. The implementation of such Internet programs and websites like social networking and blogs have changed the way that businesses communicate in an online environment. Business owners and investors must remain aware of new technologies and how they affect day-to-day business processes. Several types of B2B markets exist. In some cases, a single company will sell everything and one company completes all of the purchases. Other forms use intermediaries and private auctions with special invitation only. This can be done by the internet, intranet, and interoffice lines of communication. When businesses sell to individuals, their intended purpose is to sell a product or service with a profit, yet remain competitive. An example of a many-to-many exchange, many buyers connect electronically with many sellers and prices are negotiated for the best deal. In this form, communication is in every corner, and the selling is usually run by a third party. An example of B2B communication would be when the power company procures fuel rods, mechanical parts, and other necessary equipment from a contractor that is on site and runs the warehouse. They negotiate the price of the product, warehouse fees and personnel costs of loading or unloading the parts. From the outside, it looks like the same company, but there are actually several companies working together to run this plant. The electric consumer does not get the opportunity, or is at least restricted, to negotiate the price they pay for electricity. The closest thing they will see as far as negotiation is average billing in areas where that is an option. Basically as a consumer, they will pay for what electricity they use in their homes and businesses.

I believe dynamic pricing is fair. People make purchases due to market information that is available. If they are satisfied with the price and they feel the need to purchase a product or sell it, it is their choice. They could easily wait until the price goes down, but most people will readily accept a price and go with it. In today's economy, virtually any product can be researched, and consumers have a lot of information at their fingertips (Turban, King, McKay, Marshall, Lee & Viehland, 2008).

Proactive communication between buyers can result in a low price at auction, especially on e-bay. The problem is, there will always be that one individual who seeks to drive up the cost for the sake of competition. During the dynamic price auction, some buyers will not see other buyers; only their bid. I believe this is a way to cut down on cross-communication and allow the consumers to slowly drive the price up, but still keep it competitive. "The internet facilitates many of the dynamic pricing models for both B2B and B2C" (Turban, et al, 2008, p. 264).

Any business, online or brick-and-mortar, must have an effective supply chain. An e-supply chain can be used for businesses and is typically monitored and operated via Web technologies. E-procurement measures can be used to cut down on the need for mass amounts of paper documents and to add speed to sourcing, filling out contracts, placing orders for materials, and requesting payments for invoices. E-logistics also speeds up this process by allowing distribution channels to be streamlined (Turban, King, McKay, Marshall, Lee, & Viehland, 2008).

Several infrastructure tools are available for e-businesses. These include, "Electronic Data Interchange (EDI), Extranets, Intranets, Corporate Portals, Workflow Systems and Tools, and Groupware and Other Collaborative Tools" (Turban, et al, 2008, p. 311). Some barcodes have been replaced with Radio Frequency Identification Devices (RFID) and are used for inventory tracking and loss prevention (prevention of store theft). Corporate portals can be accessed by certain wireless devices and are utilized by customers as well as employers for specialized information retrieval (Turban, et al, 2008).

Mary,

The increase in technology has presented many problems for intellectual property owners. Congress enacted The U.S. Copyright Act, which finds its authority in the United States Constitution, Article I, Section 8, which protects the intellectual property of authors and writers (Cornell University Law School, n.d.). Different interpretations of Copyright have to be applied when working in an online environment. Companies like Napster found out how serious the artists were at protecting what was rightfully theirs. YouTube and other sites which allow uploads can be a potential problem for businesses, but they can also open themselves up for potential costly litigation in the process.

Telemedicine is meant to be an additional benefit to coincide, not replace, professional medical advice and procedures. It is strictly regulated by the Food and Drug Administration (FDA) under the provisions of the Drug and Cosmetic Act (Center for Telehealth & E-Health Law, 2009). The annual Telemedicine Trade Fair is held to focus on ways that technological advances in the medical industry can contribute to business opportunities with respect to telemedicine (Med-e-Tel, 2002). Telemedicine has provided many health professionals with new and exciting business opportunities, and has provided a platform for the introduction of new technological advancements in the medical field.

According to State of California: CA.Gov (2010), "Senate Bill 1665 requires the practitioner to obtain verbal and written informed consent (Business & Professions Code Section 2290.5) from the patient prior to delivering health care via telemedicine" (Practicing Medicine through Telemedicine Technology, para. 4). Telemedicine is not meant to be a replacement for professional medical care, but there are ways to help people by the use of technology such as the Alcatel-Lucent TeleHealth Manager; a computerized monitoring system (U.S. Department of Health & Human Services, 2009). Yes, it is very appropriate to consider telemedicine as a business opportunity, even if the healthcare professional that is utilizing this technology believes that it is his or her "calling" to do so.

Online e-auctions offer flexibility which may not be available with traditional methods. Many types of auctions exist, such as forward auctions, where many potential customers are presented with various products. With e-auctions, an enormous amount of market information is available to buyers as well as sellers about many topics related to products and services. There are complication and limitations to e-auctions. Managers must be aware of the possibility of fraud, limited participation, having the correct auction software, and other factors. Managers can eliminate or reduce these negative effects by conducting appropriate market research, essentially doing their homework to obtain knowledge about all resources available to e-auctions before staring or expanding their businesses (Turban, King, McKay, Marshall,

Lee & Viehland, 2008).

"Efficient communication is the principal device for the adequate implementation of administrative and organizational activities" (Altinöz, 2008, p. 6). I would implement a satellite video conference room where managers could meet on a daily or periodic basis to discuss organizational goals and achievements. For the employees, I would have an open-door policy to management via web-cam conference. Of course there would be telephone and inter-office email. I would send my managers a memo twice a week, and have them distribute that to all employees to make sure everyone in the company was in alignment. I would also have internet phones with software that helped the hearing impaired employees be more effective.

Explain how innovative systems are expanding communication techniques in e-commerce. Systems like e-mail, blogging, paypal, and web cams can increase the effectiveness of any business by allowing them instant access to other customers or businesses in a virtual marketplace (Turban, King, McKay, Marshall, Lee, & Viehland, 2008). We also analyzed the communication process within virtual teams. New terms this week included e-government (providing services to the private sector), C2C (consumer to consumer marketing), e-learning in virtual environments as well as continuing education, and virtual communication in general (Turban, et al, 2008). "Virtual communication technologies increase the efficiency of communication especially in virtual teams" (Altinöz, 2008, p. 6).

During the discussions, we talked about telemedicine and if it should be considered a business, since medicine has been around for so long. It appears that most of the class has decided that it should be considered a business. As an organizational manager, and being involved in the virtual workplace, I would have to consider the audience that will be receiving the information, and the content and potential impact of a virtual message. "You need to put yourself in the reader's place and decide whether your message will be favorably received, unfavorably received, or resisted" (Turban, King, McKay, Marshall, Lee & Viehland, 2008, p. 74). If you are communicating with federal agency officials or agencies, you should copy your senators, and vice-versa. Although this is not completely a virtual workplace, most communication to these officials will be by electronic means or letter correspondence.

Another instance where e-mail may be used as a medium to report to someone in the virtual workplace is when you have to deliver bad or disappointing news. Words should be wisely chosen and maintain a positive but direct tone (Turban, et al, 2008). In my opinion, delivering bad news in person is the best way; no one likes to be terminated by e-mail or text-message. When managers and business owners send information in the virtual workplace, they must protect their assets by these three critical tasks: Assess Risks, Monitor Threats to Business, and draft a Cyber Plan (NCSA, n.d.).

According to (2010), "The Health Insurance Portability and Accountability Act of 1996 provides Federal guidelines," for employers and business owners, with respect to individual privacy rules in communication and records keeping (What medical information is not covered by HIPAA, para. 1-2). Certain items are not covered by this Law, and employers should be cognizant of the specifics before transmitting certain personal documents in the workplace by electronic means. The Federal Gramm-Leach-Bliley Act (GLB) also sets guidelines for personal information and privacy rules in the workplace in regard to banks and financial institutions (2010).

Public Law 107-204 section (2) addresses audits by an independent public accounting firm, and section (8) covers other issues that the accounting firm may provide not listed in the above paragraph. It further strengthens the accounting guidelines that are proposed in the Securities Exchange Act of 1934. These issues were brought into the headlines of American news when the Arthur Anderson Accounting firm was found to be negligent in the accounting practices of the Texas-based Enron Corporation. The courts found the accounting firm guilty on numerous charges and Enron executives were not clean either. Subsequently, many investors and employees lost all or most of their retirement and investments.

Senior corporate executives are now held to a higher standard of accountability when it comes to audits and control over their companies or corporations financial structures. There will be more government oversight of the money derived from variable financial products where the public has invested their money for the growth of the said corporation. The additional oversight may create a large bureaucracy of paperwork but the checks and balances were an attempt to thwart future unscrupulous behavior in the financial sector. I do believe that when other people's money is involved, there must be appropriate action taken to protect their monetary instruments. In the big scheme of things, consumer and investor confidence has a direct correlation with the strength of the American economy. If investors believe that an organization is ethical, and has carried out their fiduciary responsibilities in a professional manner, the economy will continue to be healthy. The corporations should be operating on the up-and-up anyway, but there are always a few bad apples that ruin it for everyone else. Ethical issues and dilemmas in the business environment occur frequently. The largest threat to the business is a breach of investor trust and the loss of the consumer confidence in the business relationship. Market costs are directly affected by bad ethical decisions. With costs being bad enough, bad ethical accounting can also lead to increased government regulation, which in turn will cause companies to pass that extra cost on to the consumer, and consumers may shy away from a particular brand or commodity if the company has a marred reputation in the past with their business practices (Tyson-Chan, 2008).

Unethical accounting affects the profession by damaging the reputation of other CPA firms. Past grievances has caused an increase in the amount of ethics-related material on the Uniform CPA Examination, and if violators are found to have acted unethically, they may not be able to report or work for the SEC or report any finding to the IRS, which would subsequently limit their business potential (Romal, 2009). Managers may stop unethical accounting practices by following the generally accepted accounting principles (GAAP). Even with these guidelines in place, it is ultimately up to the individual manager to increase awareness of the severity of unethical behavior, and they must set the example to the employees that these types of violation will not be tolerated (Zarka, 2007).

Whether an individual owns his or her business or invests in publicly traded companies, they will need to know the basic accounting principles that will allow them to be organized. It is a misconception that accounting principles are reserved for the CPA (certified public accountant) or company bookkeeper. Anyone with basic knowledge of accounting principles can put that knowledge into practice in a variety of ways. Accounting can get as complex as tax-deferred status on an investment portfolio and as simple as keeping track of the family business receipts on an excel spreadsheet for further dissemination of return on investment. One such article on accounting, *"Basic Knowledge Needed for Share-Picking Process,"* asks pertinent financial analysis questions for the do-it-yourself business owner. These questions address fair and challenging issues about the financial growth potential and health of any organization (2006). To be brief, there are publically traded companies and mutual companies. Share holders buy shares of the stocks of the publically traded companies, and policy holders actually own a piece of the mutual companies. Mutual companies are not publically traded on the New York Stock Exchange, although their primary investment and financial instruments are corporate bonds. As New York Life insists on training its employees to a higher-than-normal standard of excellence, company leaders stress the fact that an investment is only as safe and strong as the company that investors choose to do business with. New York Life Insurance Company is the oldest, strongest mutual company still in operation in the United States.

One of the reasons for our success is good accounting, adequate risk management, integrity and ethical principles and good management. According to U.S. Securities and Exchange Commission (2002), [The Sarbanes-Oxley Act was established] "To protect investors by improving the accuracy and reliability of corporate disclosures made pursuant to the securities laws, and for other purposes" (para 1). The Sarbanes-Oxley Act was a direct consequence of unscrupulous business dealing by a well-known accounting firm and by unethical misconduct by a large American corporation. Although some would argue that the events surrounding Enron Corporation and the Arthur Anderson Accounting Firm marred the relationships between investors and stock-trading companies and the relationship of trust between the U.S. Government and American accounting firms, speculation exists that the accountability, reliability and integrity of the firms has been strengthened with tighter restrictions and accountability. Financial statements show the relationship between the balance sheet and income statement. They show what the company's current financial status is, and the operating results for a specific period. Included in the financial statement is a statement of cash flow, which literally tells how the company made the cash during that specific period. The dates on these papers are important, because the growth potential and financial strength of the company is judged per episode, or quarter, by invertors and those financial institutions that will be sending or receiving money from the company. The three primary items listed above tie (articulate) the strength of the company into a financial analysis that will be scrutinized by other financial experts.

A company's profit is the income minus the expenses, put simply. A company that has an enormous profit during a quarter, but also has a negative cash flow can indicate excess debt and unpaid account receivables. It can also send a signal to investors that the company spent more money than it is receiving through payment, but at the same time, it could indicate growth due to investing money in new equipment and research and development. One quarter of this condition may cause stock prices to whither, but if the company shows a profit in the next quarter, not too much worry by investors.

Examples of fixed costs in my workplace would include rent that the General Office pays to the owner of the building, E&O Insurance (liability for insurance agents), office equipment depreciation (phones, faxes, computers, copiers, etc.), and managing partner's salaries, the latter of which remains constant notwithstanding any bonus at the end of the quarters or annually. Variable costs at work may include the amount of cases and commission each agent sales (agents are paid in proportion to the amount of volume), office supplies and pre-printed forms such as life-insurance forms and attachments, and I would include utilities (Texas summers drive up an electric bill). Costs that may be variable and fixed components would be a standard office manager salary. It is usually constant but if certain expectations are met, they would receive an additional training and expense allowance and case rate bonus, which is not guaranteed. Cost-volume-profit analysis (C-V-P) can help resolve the difference in variable and fixed costs (Albrecht, Stice, & Stice, 2008).

A manager or accountant can use a C-V-P to determine how the company's sales are affecting the profit. In our organization, the managing partner will decide at the beginning of each month how many new cases the agents need to write in order to cover all expenses, including their commission payments, so the company can have a profit. This type of analysis is often overlooked by small business owners and thus causes many to fail within the first year. A company cannot "break even" and operate for an extended period of time without being forced to close its doors (Albrecht, Stice, & Stice, 2008).

Managing receivables begins with a thorough credit analysis and a plan. Term of credit as well as collection policies must be in place prior to the borrower securing the loan or line of credit. A loan or account manager must see past credit history up to and including a credit report, which is a fair indicator of whether the company or individual will be diligent enough to repay the debt. A credit manager must remember that the name of the game is to maximize profits notwithstanding a few bad accounts or loans. Management practices that tend to slow the process of collection probably began before the loan was made. This could be by a poor analysis of the person's ability to repay the debt (Albrecht, Stice & Stice, 2008).

Recent changes in banking include floating, a process that delays payment, and the use of the debit card, instead of credit cards or personal checks. Check writing has slowed because of the convenience of the plastic cards and the fact that when the debit card is used, the seller can immediately draw money electronically from the purchasers. This cuts down on the enormous backlog of hot checks, the money it takes to process checks, and the possibility that the check will not clear the bank a few days later after the merchandise has already left the premises (Albrecht, Stice & Stice, 2008).

Chapter 3 Strategies

Recently, there has been an increase in the amount of negative gossip in the workplace. Certain employees have been addressing concern over subjects ranging from politics and religion to internal family and relationship issues. Some of these issues involve the employee who is gossiping, and some do not. This is having an adverse affect on morale and is being viewed by upper level management as being a leading cause of human performance errors. Lazarus (1999) stated, "First, the importance of the coping process in emotion has been generally underestimated because the emphasis has been on appraisal" (p. 101). If this problem continues to exist, there will be a review committee set into place to look into various available tools and policies, in order to address a meaningful and responsible course of action in resolving the problem. Any information gathered on the topic of negative gossip in the workplace should only involve direct conversation. Any third party interpretation of another employee's opinion or complaints should be regarded as potential gossip in itself, or should be discarded completely. If a complaint is filed, an investigation should be initiated to determine the source of the statements. As managers, we should take into consideration not only the gossip and negative viewpoints, but the underlying source of the anxiety which exists as a catalyst for such behavior. According to Carlson (1997), most managers today would agree that the process of managing stress in the workplace is a difficult task, and that stress is indeed a fact of life with most of their employees. There will be a need to discuss the situation with the human resource department in order to insure that the problem is dealt with in a professional manner. According to Campbell (1971), individual perspectives can be limited to the experiences in which a person has been involved in, and therefore a person's viewpoints can appear to be small minded to the outside world, while presenting a huge difficulty in the life of those affected. The process that we will use to evaluate the problem will include, but not be limited to, individual counseling of all employees in the workplace, one on one interviews of workers who have been initiating the gossip, behavioral assessment in the event an employee becomes agitated or aggressive or has had a trend of antagonistic behavior which affect other employees in their immediate work area, and the installation of a step program to allow the employees the appropriate amount of time to correct their behavior if they chose to do so. "Behavioral change is difficult, but without [some kind of] support from others, it may be altogether impossible" (Gentry, 1999, p. 73). We will put an open door policy into place so every employee can address concerns about the issue without fear of retaliation or job security status. This process will investigate the validity of any complaint from the employee perspective, as well as management expectation for workplace conversation and behavior, which could ultimately jeopardize production, output, and return on investment.

After all interviews are completed and the data is processed, a meeting of all managers will occur. The final assessment may take a considerable amount of time, so we will urge management to keep all individuals involved, and all data that has been gathered in a confidential state until such time as the issues can be addressed to the workers and follow up concerns or information can be dealt with and annotated for record by the human resource department. Things that must be taken into consideration are the current state of the economy, which could affect each individual employee in a different way, and such perspectives as individual means of coping with anxiety and stress due to family issues, socioeconomic status or perceived status, possible substance abuse resulting in aberrant behavior, or social withdrawal which may be a sign of onset depression. The company will not attempt to diagnose, provide immediate treatment for, or derive a psychological assessment of any employee. If further evaluation is needed, the employee will be referred to the Employment Assistance Program or a professional in the area of stress management or mental health. Our employees are vital to our economic viability in the marketplace and their quality of life and mental well being is in the interest of company policy.

Communication Strategy

When dealing with different learning styles we need to be aware of a diverse educational situation. One particular learning style outlined by the reading assignment based on the research of Howard Gardner is the verbal/linguistic style. There are several traits associated with an individual who currently possesses this style including the ability to analyze the use of language, and being able to remember definitive terms easily. People who posses this trait are more likely to be good teachers because of the use of humor, and being able to fit that into everyday scenarios, thus convincing their students to complete a task in an enjoyable manner. This type of learner usually can read a text without excessive highlighting, and be able to rewrite notes in a clearer pattern, and is typically good at moot (debate). This is one of the areas where I scored highest while completing the multiple pathways to learning worksheet.

One strategy that I often use in communicating with a group of individuals is convincing fellow employees of the big picture when task completion is concerned. When there is a tremendous amount of negative feedback, and it appears to be affecting morale, I try to intervene with a positive message. Even my writing has a hint of humorous sarcasm which can often lighten the mood, especially when I deliver a presentation at work. A little humor can be readily received, but too much can become trite.

Another learning style is evident in the habits of the visual/spatial character. There are distinguishable mannerisms in this model that include development capabilities, usage of charts and graphs, and colorful notes when organizing thoughts. This individual can easily visualize the material that they are dealing with. They may choose direct communication with plenty of charts and visual displays, to include power point presentations to advise or teach in a group setting. I show to me moderately developed in this area. I can remember back when I served in the Army when I had to present strategies on sand tables and diagrams to my squad. It took a little preparation to try to convey my thought and the orders that I had been given to a group of people who depended on me to give them accurate instructions. Depth perception and distance were always limiting factors when dealing with models that were not drawn or constructed to scale. The third learning developmental skill that I would like to cover is the interpersonal type. This was one of the areas where I showed to be highly developed on my worksheet. Some of the abilities associated with this group are the ability to see things from someone else's perspective. This coincides with the old adage, "being able to put yourself in someone else's shoes." Cooperation with a group and being able to create and maintain lasting healthy relationships is a definite indicator of someone who possesses these intelligence features. This type is also synonymous with being highly developed in verbal, as well as non-verbal communication (Carter, Carol, Bishop, Joyce, Kravits, Sarah L., 2007). I know with working at my current position as a nuclear security officer, it is vital that I be able to read nonverbal cues when dealing with human behavior traits. I have to observe people and their actions on a daily basis, while at the same time realizing that armed guards have the ability to make people nervous, and thus we share a responsibility to always act in a professional manner consistent with plant policies and procedures. The three different personality types that I will cover in this assignment are the thinker, the organizer and the giver. While the thinker is suited best for solving problems, you can rely on the organizer to keep the project neat and sensible, while the giver will be helpful in supplying honest feedback on the project. Organizers tend to adhere to scheduling while givers will be more readily willing to use the hands on approach for a more expressive learning style.

All three styles can be essential to group success, and these are not all that exists (Gardner, Howard, 1993). Having such diversity in groups, especially in the workplace will lead to overall increases in profits and will allow the employer to more efficiently meet deadlines and quotas. Whenever I have been in a supervisor role, I have tried to interview my "hands" to see where each would be most effective. I tried to tell myself to keep in mind that an employee who is shown respect will reciprocate that respect, and the lines of communication will remain open. Formal writing will always have a place in the business world. Correspondence that is sent interoffice will need to be in a clear, concise manner in order to keep businesses running smoothly with very little margin for error. Texting a message to a friend or co-worker has become an acceptable method of conveying information, but it has had a substantial impact on sentence structure and fluidity in my opinion. Also, it is good to have follow up communication and to be serious, a thank you note will go a long way to improving business relations. I suppose a digital thank you note would suffice, but I prefer "snail mail." Writing has been used in the past to communicate an individual's thoughts in prose, as compared to symbols, which were used prior to a structured language being adopted by a given society. By using cell phones and text messages, we shortcut the given information and thus rely on the receiver to interpret our tone and intent. While useful, these media options often lead to misinterpretation and misinformation, leading to clarification and explanation which can cost us extra time, when picking up the phone and relaying our message would have been the best choice in the first place. One rule of thumb; if your message sounds unclear when you read it to yourself, don't send it.

My teenage step-daughter does not consider texting to be writing. This is an example of how texting is perceived and how writing is perceived. She has explained that texting is a random way to get a quick message out to a friend, kind of an answer to a quick question. When it comes to writing, her and her friends consider that when an assignment is given at school, and they have to actually "turn in" a paper to their teacher, then at that point, it is considered writing. Also, as a manager, don't be an "empty suit" and come out of your office only to correct your minions.

Chapter 4

Professional Values and Ethics

In order for an individual to be successful and competitive in today's marketplace, they will not only have to be well educated in business policies and tactics, but they must attain a high level of integrity and ethical behavior. Gone are the days where unscrupulous dealings can be overlooked by regulatory agencies and unprofessional behavior viewed as commonplace in the work environment. The relationship between a person's value system, their ethical standards in both their business and private lives, and their professional success is a testament to the increasing quality and standards which are expected in a trustworthy business atmosphere.

According to Clarkson (2009), ethics can be defined as the study of what is right and what is wrong, and the different views on the subject by a given society. Sources for ethical standards can range from biblical references and views on moral conduct and behavior to regulations set forth in a given state or society which have been agreed upon by that society or a majority of its people. The United States Government (2009) Web site outlines Federal Ethics Laws as a source of professional ethics which the Department of Transportation requires all employees to be in compliance. These laws address employee conduct and specific standards applicable to her job specifications, and the DOT also provides the standards of Ethical Conduct as a guide for their employee's duties and responsibilities. Ethical conduct can also be handed down through family members and elders in the community as a guide for the youth, and as instruction and wisdom which can only be attained from mistakes, misgivings, and lessons learned through time.

To describe how professional ethics may affect success in a positive or negative way, consider the end result of impropriety. In today's marketplace, an unethical decision by a Chief Operating Officer of a major corporation can negatively affect that corporation's interests, return on investment, viability ion the marketplace, and employee job security. Another example could be in a case of employee theft, which will affect morale, trust, and ultimately affect the employee relationship with the company, most likely resulting in termination of employment.

According to Soccio (2007), the works by Danish philosopher Soren Kierkegaard (1813-1855) revealed ethics as an actual stage of a person's life. He stated that an ethical life was devoted to certain general principles, and that every man or woman chooses weather to live by an ethical code. Peters (2007) stated,"[That] All the mathematical and economic capabilities in the world and all the substantive knowledge of policy areas are of little consequence if we have no moral or ethical foundation on which to base our evaluation of policies" (p. 450). This quote shows the importance of ethics even in the government policy making arena. Professional ethics affects every person from the individual mechanic in a shop to the CEO of a company, and especially as high up as the President of the United States. A few former presidents have made unethical decisions which affected not only their ratings, but the trust in their office by the American people as well as the foreign view of their integrity (Democrat as well as Republican or any other party). A sense of right or wrong and a background in ethical decision making can make everyday decisions reliable and consistent. In conclusion, professional ethics are important to every facet of the economy in order to provide a trustworthy platform on which the marketplace can achieve vitality and so it may provide the essential heartbeat on which a capitalistic society can thrive. An economy devoid of ethics and professional conduct will in fact, break down upon itself through mistrust and collapse under the load of complaints and lawsuits associated with such behavior. A high standard of ethical standard, as demonstrated by the requirements of the Department of Transportation for its employees, or by the philosophical beliefs and aspirations laid out by earlier thinkers, and by the elders in a given society which have provided instruction for younger generations will no doubt be the foundation of a society where a sense of right or wrong can continue to be paramount. To summarize briefly, ethical behavior can be simplified into what is perceived and believed to be right or wrong, and the study thereof. Ethical behavior has been addressed for many years through the writings and policies of past civilizations, and by such philosophers as Aristotle and Plato. Ethical conduct will continue to be of utmost importance to the proper execution of government policy and for the economic health of countries who seek to be viable in the global marketplace.

Professional ethics are similar to personal ethics by the nature of what is expected to happen even when there is no one around to scrutinize the behavior. In a professional environment, a client expects the professional to act in such a manner where trust and reliability cannot be compromised and where confidentiality is sought after as the regular order of business. Basically, what is right and fair and how we operate as professionals is how we would operate in our own lives when no one is looking; it is just the right thing to do. A work environment is more pleasing to the employee and the business owner when everyone acts in an ethical manner in that the duties and requirements of most professions do not allow for any failure in integrity and honesty which costs companies extra man-power in loss-prevention and over-checking of work-related incidents. If employees can be trusted, there is little need for follow up direction and security breach contingency plans.

Ethics Awareness Inventory Analysis

According to the ethics awareness inventory, I base my ethical perspective on what it is to be, in contrast to good behavior. The inventory explained that I put a lot of emphasis on moral excellence and that I believe people should try harder to achieve moral excellence. I agree with that assessment. It found that I scrutinize an individual's character. That could be because I hold myself to a higher standard and I expect the same from everyone else. Our textbook outlines that, "The focus of ethics is moral situations," (Ruggiero, 2008, p. 5). I don't just look at the situation, but the person as well. The old adage "actions speak louder than words" comes to mind.

According to the aforementioned inventory, my profile in regards to ethics is more aligned with character than that of end results. A person's character speaks volumes. I believe that a man or woman is known by their friends, and it is a direct reflection of who they are and what they want to become as an individual. Even the Bible says that bad company corrupts a person's good morals. Whether someone is religious or not, that speaks volumes to me when I try to decide what is right and what group of friends I want to be associated with. My ethics assessment shows my belief in the ethics of the individual in final decision making abilities.

Professional Development

In my professional development, I am at a stage in my life where I am in a professional environment and I am expected to act ethically, be forthcoming and act honesty in the financial sector and insurance industry. This could be defined as doing the right thing when no one is around to check up on me because that is the way I was trained and that is the way I believe we should conduct business at my company. Signatures and initials are very important to the insurance industry. I have had to make a second trip to a client's home to obtain a signature or initial on a document and there is no way I would fudge paperwork. In the past, clients have asked agents to go ahead and sign their name to save them a trip, but we will not allow that at our company. It is the little things like that which can cause big trouble for a company if the field agents act in an unethical manner. My ethical statement is, "Let your conscious be your guide and integrity be your watchword." I tell that to anyone who will listen because perhaps I can be a good influence to those around me at work and in my personal life.

Conflict Resolution

I address conflict of ethical perspectives like I address any problem. I always try to think that God is watching my every move, kind of like a hidden camera. That way, I always do the right thing and I can sleep easy at night. At a previous job, I worked security at a nuclear power plant. Everything we did on a daily basis was scrutinized by the NRC (Nuclear Regulatory Commission). That job was easy for someone like me who enjoys moral values and ethical behavior, but there were times when certain employees did not follow the rules. Subsequently, I helped escort those individuals from plant property.

In summary, ethical decision-making makes for a better society. As the inventory showed, I hold these values to a high standard. I not only expect others to act in an ethical manner, but I hold myself to high ethical standards as well.

Effective decision-making is a process that involves risk assessment, first-hand knowledge of a subject and insight on the possible repercussions of actions that we encounter during the decision-making. I like to take time to analyze a problem before making a rash decision; I prefer delayed judgment. That is why the court system seems to take so long to process a trial. There needs to be a cooling off period so each side can argue their case and all of the facts can be seen or heard. Critical thinking does not involve the quick actions of a tyrant, rather the knowledgeable mind of a philosopher. Leaders in our history have often reflected on their good and best decisions being the ones that have taken the longest to make. That is not to say in a contingency situation or survival situation that we cannot make good decision that can save our lives, but in day-to-day operations, critical thinking must be implored and exhibited by all leaders and managers. At times we may be involved in a decision where others are affected by the outcome. Without critical thinking, we are not only limiting ourselves and our abilities, but we may be causing harm to others and our society. Any effective decision must be based on facts, intended outcome, and an assessment of the possible repercussions. Our short-term goals tend to skew our decision-making process in regard to accumulation of wealth or satisfying a primal need or secondary want. Short-term financial planning tends to be aggressive and dangerous, though for many, the pay-off is somewhat rewarding. In contrast, long-term planning tends to be more thoughtful and conservative, and driven by the "big picture." It will be the same in most cases; the big picture must drive our ambitions. An effective short-term analysis of school work would be to study and cram for the next test to receive a passing grade. In the long-run, if we study a little each day, we will retain that information and it may be used at a later date in an appropriate setting to allow us to be effective managers. Short-term goals have their place in our lives. If we started college and worried only about receiving a degree, we would miss out on the opportunities and experiences along the way. We must create a balance between short and long-term goals in order to survive in this day and age. I have always had a "five-year" plan; that is to say where I intend to be in the next five years. My short-term goals in combination with my dreams and wants help to balance the workloads to get me where I need to be.

Chapter 5

Professional Workplace Dilemma

At a previous job, I worked as a security supervisor at a nuclear power plant. All total, there were 4 supervisors (including myself) and a lieutenant. At times, things went smoothly and the workforce pulled together as a team and accomplished all expectations and goals. Toward the end of my duration as a supervisor, things began to take a change for the worse. Management began to falsely accuse subordinates over petty occurrences and the other supervisors began to take sides and bicker amongst themselves. This created a hostile work environment and the employees began to notice, as well as morale in the whole company decreasing on a daily basis.

From my standpoint, things got so bad that I sought other employment. I was enrolled with the University of Phoenix at the time. The supervisors that I worked with even made remarks about my education and the fact that I would be stuck at that plant forever. I did stick it out for seven years, but I finally told them that I had found a new position. Of course, I caught flack over leaving too, but it was the best decision that I ever made in regard to employment. There was a difference in perceived power, underlying innuendos, and the actual power on paper that the supervisors held in contrast to management. Employees made several attempts to rectify the situation during closed-door meetings with the Project Manager, but those meetings were not fortuitous. The worst managers believed they had more power than was actually given to that position and they abused that position on a daily basis. This was a very unethical individual; up to and including harassment of female employees. Management ethics and my fellow supervisors tactics were both in question. I found it hard to go to work every day when I knew that I would be caught in the cross-fire of some debate about who hated who, and who had acted unprofessionally. It got to the point that I hated my own job.

After a time, I knew things were not going to change without some upper echelon intervention, so I began to ask myself if I could support an organization that allowed that behavior to continue. I believed that it was just a matter of time before an EEOC complaint was brought up and the company would face unnecessary litigation; I wanted no part of that. If I would have stayed, I would potentially be held liable for not bringing up the situation to the human resources manager. The human resource manager just happened to be good friends with the lieutenant, so I felt that I would be wasting my time with that approach. The employees that I left behind probably still suffer the treatment and harassment that I witnessed, provided those individuals are still working there.

Evaluation

After several meetings about the individual with questionable ethics, and no response from the Project Manager, of course, I left the company to work for a better-respected company where I could go to sleep at night with a clear conscious. Given all that I have learned from my experiences, I would only change one thing; I should have left sooner. Those individual's behavior started to affect my outlook on life and my personality. I started being short-tempered and had feelings that people did not like the job I was doing because I always tried to be political and not cause waves at work. This made it look like I had no opinion at all, but on the contrary, I did not agree at all with that kind of behavior. I believe that I am more aware of workplace conditions and that if this problem existed in another company, I would know the correct course of action to take.

Anytime someone, especially a manager acts in an unethical way at work, it says a lot about them as a person. They are leaders, and they should try to set a good example for the employees, which will in turn benefit everyone involved. This includes employees, shareholders, stakeholders and investors. My evaluation of my decision-making process goes back to the way I was raised. Do the right thing and treat others as you want to be treated. If all managers held those simple values, there would be no problems at the workplace.

The class that had the most influence on my future studies was Introduction to Psychology. It was the first class that I took at a real college. I had previously taken a government class while in the military, but that was a totally different setting, and less enjoyable. After years of letting college be at the back of my mind, I enrolled in a community college with Psychology and Algebra. The Psychology teacher was very good, and she helped me realize a lot about human behavior and what I was thinking when I started my studies. It sparked my interest in school, new books, learning, and education in general. Through that semester, I read so many books at the school library; it was like I began to have an insatiable appetite for learning. It was probably that class, though it was also just a point in my life when I was ready for a change. Throughout the next few years following that course, I had to deal with human behavior at work and deal with different personalities. That class allowed us to analyze our personality types and find ways to deal with our own biases and decision making abilities. This really helped in the "real world" and in the job environment. One barrier that comes to my mind is anxiety. If we worry too much how others will perceive us, we may never reach our full potential. That can be true in both personal and professional lives. Our personal growth depends on many factors, such as education, experiences, and in the far reaches of the spectrum, even loss. Yes, when we experience loss, such as a loved one or loss of a treasure that we hold deep, we must find a way to adapt and overcome, and that causes us to grow on a personal level. If we fail to adapt properly, we can regress to a stage that will take us a long time to recover from.

Our growth and development may come from our extrinsic motivating factors such as a promotion at our career, or leaving our present career for a more challenging one. Some would argue that it shows loyalty to stay at a job 20-30 years and then retire. In my own opinion, that may be good for some people, but for me, I have had several jobs and I see it as a means to grow and adapt to a new and challenging situation. In the past, I felt like I stayed way too long at a dead-end career, and the only way to get promoted was to actually leave the company. I have never been one to think that I am not replaceable, because business will go on and continue to operate, but I knew that I needed a change for my own personal growth and development.

Chapter 6 Past, Present, and Future

I would describe management as a diverse group of people who have been tasked to provide supervision, control and guidance to a specific workforce. Their primary goal would be to achieve the objectives set by their particular company or organization in order to make a profit in that business, or in the case of a non-profit organization, their goal would be to maintain the processes which are the vision and scope of that organization. Management is necessary in order for the company to accomplish goals and objectives, make decisions on a daily basis, and insure that there is proper communication from the top to the bottom in the business structure. Managers are directly involved with the fundamental decision making of any business.

There are four management functions, including planning, organizing, leading and controlling. A business would not operate smoothly without proper planning. The organizing of a business is vital so that each member of the team knows what is expected of them, and they can execute their duties to the fullest extent of their abilities. All businesses must have a leader, otherwise, the people involved would wander around in many directions and no goals would be accomplished. Controls are set in place to maintain focus and ensure common thoughts and achievements, which believe it or not always go back to making a profit for the company. Businesses would fail if they continued to operate without making a profit, and managers are tasked to make decisions while keeping that in mind.

Management has evolved in many ways such as the way they treat people now compared to 50 or 100 years ago. With the Industrial revolution, changes in management became more of a science or an art, and not simply an example of trying something and seeing if it failed, then moving on to the next mistake. There used to be problems in communication between boss and worker (there still is sometimes), adverse working conditions, and transportation limitations which caused many businesses to stop growing, which in turn reduced return on investment. According to one website, the modern model of business originated with the practices and tactics of Sir Thomas More (1478-1535), so you can see managers have been taking a hard look at how to plan and organize a business for many years.

Management will continue to be a process that is used to complete business goals, and will help organizations meet the global demands that are placed on them today in the marketplace. There are several ways in which effective management can impact the overall success of an organization. One way is by ensuring that a company stays current and operates within the guidelines of the laws and regulations which are set in place. The power plant where I work is regulated by the Nuclear Regulatory Commission, and not only the licensee must comply with NRC mandates, but all contractors as well. The United States Government places strategic constraints on different companies; but they also may provide opportunities for that company by decreasing competition to only those companies who are under their regulations.

Organizational success also affects the overall growth and strength of the national economy. As individuals form companies, which become corporations and larger entities, the need for a good management team becomes vital to ensure the employees are taken care of, and to ensure all requirements are met in order for the company to continue to grow in today's changing market environment. Now more importantly, corporations must be ready to survive in a global atmosphere and by doing so, they need to ensure that the right managers are in place to execute that process. The bottom line in the business world is that the organization is only as strong as its weakest link, and hopefully that does not turn out to be the management team.

Personally, I feel the most important aspect of the function of a manager is to keep in mind the people who have brought the company their success. It is true that bottom line profit margins are the reason any company continues to operate, but if the workforce is neglected, profits will suffer and the company may in fact break down due to morale issues and internal struggles. Management must pay attention to cost saving measures because of increased competition, but the employee well-being must be in the picture to a certain degree. They must also take into consideration the education level of their employees, as technological shortcomings will not be an asset in an evolving marketplace. If employees are lacking in certain technological skills, it will be up to the management team to train them and get them up to speed. They must also take into account an ageing, ailing workforce while at the same time evaluating those older employees for the experience that they provide to a company.

Chapter 7

Organizational Philosophies and Technology

Companies can use current technology to assist their respective departments in managing ethical standards and guidelines. One of the ways they can accomplish this task is by creating a procedure or policy that addresses proper implementation while employees are in the online environment. Firewalls can be used to create a barrier between the user and the recipient, and can help deter phishing and data mining. Internal communication can be protected by using the "layering" technique, which is primarily set up by the internet security or Internet technology (IT) departments. Ethics boils down to doing the right thing and doing it even if there appears to be no one watching. The right thing may include not using profanity in an e-mail or by using tact on the phone while conducting a customer service call. Most people believe they want to do a good job, but for those who are not quite as strict about their behavior, a guideline or restriction must be put in place for management oversight. Extranets can help managers control data that is exchanged between two individuals and it actually cuts down on extra software requirements. Copyright infringement and piracy are two areas of concern in today's technology based business environment. The music business, by far, has been the industry most hit by the copying of compact disks (CD) and sharing music by downloading. Copyright laws are and ethical and legal guideline set forth to protect a creator's right to their product, and to protect companies form litigation as a result of a complaint by various users of that technology. These laws limit the user to tight restrictions concerning new and currently used software. For example, a company may purchase Microsoft 7 Operating System, but they may have to purchase additional licenses for each computer that the software will be install don. That way, a company can't just by one CD and upload it to several computers and have only purchased one product (Reagan & O'Conner, 2002). Ethical guidelines are put in place to help shape the culture of a company. If the employees know that their respective employer "plays by the rules," they will be less likely to commit ethical infractions in their daily work. The top of the management hierarchy is where honesty, integrity and an ethical approach to good decision-making start. Employees will generally follow the rules and guidelines set by company management (Reagan & O'Conner, 2002).

Human resources can use technology to save employee data and to assess the quality of current employees. There are rules and ethical guidelines that help the human resource departments in insurance companies and they are based on a code of ethics. These guidelines affect not only the company and agent in the field, but also protect the consumer or client form unethical business practices. One such safeguard is to have as many third-party players in the writing of a policy to maintain integrity and honesty in the underwriting process (Kensicki, 2010).

In 2002, President George W. Bush signed the Sarbanes-Oxley Act into law. This law was a direct result of unethical decisions and business practices by the Arthur Anderson Accounting Firm, which subsequently turned into the Enron scandal. At the time, financial professional were thought to possess a great deal of integrity and were seldom regulated to the extent they are today. Computer technology and the up-to-the-minute updates from Wall Street make it hard for investors and professionals to "cook the books" as was done in previous years. The detrimental effect that this scandal produced was monumental to tighter regulations in the financial industry. There will always be dishonesty in any venture as all people are not wise and forthcoming. For those that obey the laws of the land, they can rest peacefully at night knowing that they are conducting business in a professional and ethical manner. In contrast, for those who wish to abuse the laws and the system, they will eventually get caught and brought to justice. In the big scheme of things, a little dishonesty in any business only raises prices that punish the consumers and the whole economy van be affected if the scandal ids large enough (Ewing, n.d.).

Managers have at their disposal many tools in order to design and implement an ethically based model for their business. Trade-offs may include bonuses for those that are found to be in strict compliance and for those employees that seek a culture of honesty and integrity in their business practices. Managers must evaluate the problems and reach a solution if change is ever going to occur in their model (, n.d.).

It is no secret that technology is growing and developing faster than most of us can comprehend. For those individuals that make or create the technology, they face competition from the next line of highly sophisticated inventions. This causes stress in the workplace, but that is for another discussion. Technology is essentially a set of new tools that we as humans must master or at least overcome in order to remain viable components of a futuristic global environment, and for those who allow the technology to pass them by, they will be at a disadvantage in the marketplace. At one time, the John Deere plow was top of the line technology for producing crops. That has since been improved upon, and crops are grown by more of a scientific method. The use of technology to sustain our lives is a testament to what man or woman ids capable in this modern age. We have so many resources at our disposal that we sometimes lose the human touch in our business practices. Thank you cards have been replaced by a mass e-mail to our customer base (Gil, n.d.).

To some company owners, profit is the only incentive to their continued success. Public relations companies are making a killing because the companies are actually detaching themselves from the client base and would rather outsource the "feel good" moments that are associated with new technology and products. As far as ethics are concerned, it all boils down to the one thing we all have but seldom use properly; individual choice (Ethisphere Magazine, 2010).

In summary, the human element is still essential in the implementation of new technology. Until that time comes where the machine can thing autonomously, customer service departments will still be a valuable asset to the individual consumer and the technology inventors will continue to produce new gadgets to help the world.

Chapter 8

The Function of Management

The function of management is not to be an overlord. The function of management is not to see how hard they can make the lives of their subordinates. The function of management is not to allow their subordinates to cry out during a meeting only to find ways to secretly abuse their power over the subordinate in a later workplace situation. The function of a manager is not to sit proudly behind a chair and after misconstruing a situation and totally blowing it out of proportion making the employee feel less than human asking that employee if they have anything to add. This while leaning forward looking at the employee as a hungry tiger looks at a t-bone steak. No, the four functions of management which provide managers with the ability to act ethically and effectively are planning, organizing, leading and controlling. The business atmosphere is changing at an increasing pace, and this requires managers to adapt to these changes with all resources available. Global challenges have been noticed and addressed in management, and these present challenges as well as opportunities for organizations to be competitive and profitable. Adapting to change will allow managers to grow on a personal level, and it will provide a means for older organizations to bring themselves up to speed with technology and innovation. Communication methods have changed over the past several years and the approach in which management addresses employee concerns. A manager can implement the four main functions as a systematic approach to creating a learning style which will address a diverse and technologically educated workforce. As new methods of management are realized, older methods can be modified to provide a standard of quality which will increase profits and ensure a quality product (Bateman & Snell, 2007). Management processes are defined as controlling or guiding workers, having charge of a particular process, or succeeding in doing a given task. Management is the means of toiling amidst a group in society in order to fulfill a design, group or provision. Effective managers discharge their responsibilities adequately, persuasively and respectfully. In the systematic approach to decision making, managers must be cognizant of many variables which could ultimately affect completion of a goal or profits for the company. In the course of production and distribution, management must be able to adapt to change at an alarming rate to satisfy the needs of the customer, keep expenses below satisfactory levels, and provide a nurturing atmosphere for the employees, one devoid of hostility and discrimination in order to stay within the guidelines of the law and allow for increased production. The face of business management is changing and managers must be able to accept this fact. Kilmann (1989) stated, "...constant change on the outside requires constant change on the inside" (p. 2). The four basic utilitarian concepts that managers can use as tools to provide an effective means of communication and analysis assist them in completing their everyday tasks. The first of these tools is planning. Planning is defined as devising a scheme for doing something or to have a thing in mind, such as a project or purpose. Effective planning involves gathering a wealth of knowledge, doing prior research, and implementing a device that will help accomplish goals and help the management team stay within given parameters (Bateman & Snell, 2007). Phillips and Bonner (2000) indicated that there may be a need for Chief Knowledge Officers in companies to ensure all needed resources have been gathered, and effective planning will be able to integrate the new technologies which will help managers take the appropriate course of action. A company's goals will be effective if they are aligned with the company's vision and if managers have planned appropriately to direct their tasks to meet a shared model.

The second foundational mechanism that is crucial to a manager's responsibility is organizing. Organizing is simply the collecting of available resources including personnel, monetary, and actual information in order to reach specific goals (Bateman & Snell, 2007). Weinstein (1996) stated, "Every business has its own internal culture...that becomes instantly obvious to a new employee" (p. 43). The way a business organizes its employees to perform a task may differ slightly from the next business, but in reality, organization is apparent at every level. The third function of management is leading, or motivating employees to perform at high levels in their specified duties. Leading incorporates effective communication with group interaction so that managers may relay their expectations and avoid the pitfalls of misunderstanding

(Bateman & Snell, 2007). Controlling, the final function, regulates the performance of changes in organizational goals, and ensures a quality product is being made available to the consumer. Companies have guidelines in place and must adhere to government regulations to implement quality and safety procedures properly (Bateman & Snell, 2007). In summary, the four functions of management are tools which guide managers in their decision making process. These tools provide the platform for addressing issues as well as preparation for helping a business run smoothly and efficiently. Certain processes have been developed over the years to enhance the role that management plays in the interaction with employees, and these processes will continue to be adapted to fit the changing landscape of the business environment. Situational analysis begins the planning process. This is when planners gather all available information that pertains to the issue at hand. The gathering of such information allows planners to decide the correct course of action and to forecast any future trends (a general direction or tendency) applicable to the situation. It is also at this time when planners will go over past studies related to the new situation. At the plant where I am employed, a group of planners will spend months gathering engineering feedback and reports, as well as regulatory affairs consultants to seek the appropriate method for completing a project. The primary purpose for this is to ensure strict compliance with the Nuclear Regulatory Commission and to maintain a high degree of safety for all involved.

Alternative goals and plans are used by planners to develop an alternate means of completing a project. This allows more flexibility and provides a back-up plan for any "what-if" scenarios that may arise such as budget cuts, unavailability of resources, downsizing of essential personnel, or time constraints. The nuclear plant in Texas has implemented certain contingency plans such as EP, or Emergency Planning group to initiate a response in case of emergency. Security and other operations have plans in place for such events, but are confidential in nature. Managers will evaluate goals and plan evaluation to monitor and predict any advantages or disadvantages to the plan. These goals will be prioritized and some will be removed according to need. This usually will deal with cost and time evaluations, and even personnel. Studies may be conscripted to ensure the plan is going according to cost and within budget requirements. Other methods are goal and plan selection, implementation (actually putting the project into working status), monitoring of the ongoing, repetitive process to ensure quality and reliability, and control measures. Control measures used by my current employer are QA (Quality and Assurance) supervisors, who must sign off certain tasks before the next task can be completed to provide a reliable means of peer-checking throughout the plant involving work orders. There are also supervisory limits on how much time outage workers can spend inside of certain areas of the plant to limit exposure to radiation and heat. These limits are addressed in the outage planning weeks and months prior to the work being completed.

The planning process can be affected in many ways. A combination of external and internal forces can cause the need for an alternative action plan, or goals adjustment to be implemented to deal with such issues. During this time, an examination will occur to diagnose existing as well as new problems which affect the on-going project. The second item affecting the planning process will be the evaluation of the advantages and disadvantages of the prior goals and which will be selected or eliminated. Resources will also be allocated as well as budget requirements and parameters. The third item is the installation of control systems which will monitor completing methods and actualization of the goals which have been set into place. These three major factors impact the planning process by the time it takes to evaluate and implement them, and also the current budget allowances for such research which affects the overall cost of the project. Organizational responsibility has changed over the past few decades. With recent scandals involving high level executives and politicians, as well as other key personnel, a focus on ethical behavior is paramount. Each organization is different in terms of ethical decision making approaches. While some organizations require strict compliance to ethics rules, others may tend to bend the rules occasionally, which can lead to enormous uproars in the end. There is an increase in the amount of organizations that are adopting ethics codes, and are becoming more aware of the potential side-effects of complacency in this area. Making decisions based on ethical and moral principles requires an innate ability to see how these decisions will and have affected business integrity and profit margins due to loss of time during investigations and legal costs if a complaint is filed. There is a responsibility that corporate entities must take into consideration which goes beyond just turning a profit, but how that corporation is being viewed by the outside world in terms of ethical operating behavior. If a corporation is perceived as being forthcoming and ethical, then shareholders will have more trust in the corporation. Shareholder trust will inherently affect market viability and trading profits, but the most important reason that ethics should be involved in the planning process is it eliminates the need to answer tough questions after a project is already in the implementation phase. The week two lecture explains how Benchmarking is the process in which a company learns how to become the best in its' particular industry. If they follow the guidelines of other companies which have made ethically responsible decisions, then everyone involved will profit. One example of an organizational resource is the organization chart, which shows the different positions and levels of authority in a particular business, how they are arranged, and who answers to who at what level. It also outlines the various activities that are given to individuals and what they are responsible for. During the hiring process at our company, we were required to learn the entire organizational chart which also had photos on it, in order to be able to recognize upper level management when they arrived on the plant site. Another resource example is differentiation, which explains how an organization is composed of many different units. A third resource example is Integration, which is when the differentiated units are brought back together to reach a common goal. Organizations begin to allocate scarce resources in a competitive environment by accumulating the right resources and people. Without the right people for the job, or the right equipment or machinery to make a product, the company will not have a good product to sell to the consumer. Managers can profit by allowing more responsibility to be given to their employees in order to complete different tasks, and it also allows the employee to become a more active member of the organization. Next, by putting the resources together in various ways, it gives them more avenues of approach when dealing with problems for their customers. Finally, they exploit their resources in order to use them to their fullest extent.

Organizations can ensure that their resources are allocated in accordance with their objectives by forming strategic alliances. This is a formal relationship which is formed with likeminded companies or other organization that can help a company reach its goals and production objectives. That would be like Microsoft forming a strategic alliance with a plastic company to provide the outer shells of computers, and in turn receiving discounted software from Microsoft to run the injection molding machines (it's more complicated than that, but that is just a hypothetical example). Organizations must keep current on new technology and not rely on their past achievements as indicators of future success in the marketplace if they are to remain a viable competitor. Some experts claim that the only way for a business to survive is to learn faster than the competition, which opens the door for a learning organization. This is where a company, corporation or business acquires all knowledge available and modifies its behavior accordingly to keep up with innovations and trends. Some entities have even formed task forces and are opening positions for Chief Knowledge Officers in their organizations. Management's role in organizing human capital is simply to use an employee's knowledge and skills in a way that will profit the company to the fullest. It is the duties of the Human Resource department to provide the employer with the qualified personnel and to ensure those personnel are being used in an effective way. The reading refers to human capital as intellectual capital. This describes how an employee who is more highly trained and knowledgeable about their job can benefit the company in terms of good decision making and that employee will often help teach other employees what they have learned.

This role may vary from company to company in that certain jobs require different criteria for the individual employee, and there are certain jobs that require the employee to accept more responsibility at their level. Keeping these employees knowledgeable on their assigned tasks is one thing, but it may also be important to keep them aware of changing conditions within the company as a whole in order to make them aware of the big picture. At the plant where I am employed, managers from all different departments, and even contractors attend a weekly meeting to ensure that everyone is on the same page and aware of any condition that may affect their particular job.

Human capital is the life line of all businesses. Without workers who carry out orders from managers, and managers who carry out designs and project from upper level management, no company would be in operation. There appears to be an increasing awareness of the importance of the individual worker and their specific job training skills in today's workplace. I am fortunate to work for a company that keeps these things in mind and insist on employees taking on more responsibility as the need arises. I have worked in jobs before where you were expected to do as the boss instructed, and never question an order. In the military, at times this is practical. There were times when I had a good suggestion but never thought to bring it to my supervisor's attention for fear of retaliation or losing my job. It was always disappointing when the order turned out to be a wrong decision and of course the blame started to run downhill, when the problem could have been avoided if the boss would have been open to suggestions.

Chapter 9 Management Planning

Abstract

A large accounting firm experienced a time of growth during the Great Depression and after two World Wars, only to meet its demise in the 1990s. The firm of Arthur Anderson and Company had been indicted on grounds of witness tampering, corruption, ethics violations and a plethora of other alleged offenses. Headquartered in Chicago, Illinois and with their principle operations in Houston, Texas, the aforementioned company was basically dismantled allowing its consulting firm to become a separate division from the parent company.

The Tuck (2002) Web site stated that The Anderson, DeLany and Company accounting firm was founded in 1913 by Arthur Anderson and Clarence DeLany. DeLany soon left Arthur Anderson and Company, as it is known today. This company was formed with the intent of addressing the filings and accountability caused by an increase in government regulation. As early as 1928, they began expanding their consulting practice, subsequently increasing their foothold on American accounting practices. The company continued to experience growth, and in 1963 it began serving business needs overseas. When a company is able to expand and operate in a foreign land it is a sign of growth and expansion, but also adds responsibility to the management department. The owner and visionary of this massive operation, Arthur

Anderson, died in 1947, leaving behind a firm that was steady and forthcoming, apparently unaware of the bad times that lingered in the distance for his company. His replacement was a man by the name of Leonard Spacek who was able to ease tensions and calm most inside arguments within the firm and bring the company forward to compete as one of the major accounting firms operating in the global market. The little company that began in 1913 had risen to the level of exceeding $9.3 billion in revenues by 2001. Tuck (2002).

After Arthur Anderson passed away, his replacement sought to organize the company to meet the growing demands of businesses. It was evident at the time that a restructuring of the operation procedures was in order to keep the company competitive. A situational analysis (this term may not have been used back then) involved finding out which businesses were in need of accounting services, what competitors if any were presently operating in the mainstream business climate, and if demands could be met with the current management and personnel. Evaluating the planning function of Arthur Anderson and Company management would turn out to be an arduous task, but it would also launch that company into the top five accounting firms in the world. In order to make future planning and controlling effective, management is required to keep accounting records of their past operations and the results of past evaluations of their companies by using such accounting firms as AA&C, and they can only rely on the credentials and reputations of the accounting firms that they hire (Pickle and Abrahamson, 1983). Arthur Levitt, who presided as Chairman of the SEC for eight years, sought to reform the accounting industry in America with unsatisfactory results. He stated that "If investors lose confidence in the reliability of numbers that are presented to them, our markets will suffer grievously..." Mr. Levitt wanted it to be clear that it would be more difficult to raise money through investors if the whole accounting business had become corrupt, and maintaining public interest in the stock market would be more difficult. With a loss of oversight and unethical decision making in accounting, Levitt believed that sources of capital for investment and growth would cease to exist. Arthur Anderson Company had been hired as the chief accounting firm for the Enron Energy Corporation principally based in Houston, Texas. With accusations of paper shredding and hindering a government investigation, AA&C was found guilty of such crimes and Enron collapsed leading to an inside scandal of its own. Everyone involved in the Enron investigation was at least a little bit responsible for the failure of Arthur Anderson Accounting including the board of directors, audit committee, lawyers and also the bankers. (PBS, 1998).

As an alternative goal, and one that would impose stiff regulations on companies, CEO's, and upper level management in accounting and oversight firms, a unanimous vote by the SEC in 2002 proposed new rules enhancing the reliability and integrity of the financial reporting process. This was an action by the Commission to try and repair public trust in such firms, and ease public skepticism which can directly affect the way money is invested in our economy. The new regulations created the framework for a Public Accountability Board involving a process that would not be under the control of the accounting profession, but by a separate entity. The primary purpose of the board is to easily detect deficiencies in accounting methods and ethical improprieties, and ultimately will work along side of the SEC

(Securities and Exchange Commission, 2002).

The indictment of the Arthur Anderson Accounting firm shows how the effect that lack of transparency could have on management and shareholders of a publicly traded company. It raised the awareness to accounting firms that if you shred or destroy evidence that is essential to an investigation, you could face serious criminal charges. The Arthur Anderson Company was fined and place on five years' probation which will cause more scrutiny by the government and the SEC. "The problems a business will face if it has insufficient records to justify its income tax returns are common knowledge" (Pickle & Abrahamson, 1983, p. 401). Even back in the eighties, businesses were aware of the potential repercussions of unethical accounting situations.

In 2002, President George W. Bush signed The Sarbanes-Oxley Act into law as a response to the conviction of Arthur Anderson Company and as a guide for future corporate social responsibility. Arthur Anderson and Company found itself in trouble for not properly reporting the balance sheets for the Enron Corporation, which was dismantled for insider trading and unscrupulous accounting practices. The General Accepted Accounting Principles (GAAP) basically says that a company must add in to their balance sheets all investment partnerships that exceed 3% of its total worth (United States General Accounting Office 2001). Enron exceeded this percentage, and the accounting firm of Arthur Anderson was well aware of this discrepancy, but chose to hide the details. According to GAAP, this accounting firm should have recalculated the earnings made by Enron. At the time, Arthur Andersen and Company was considered to be one of the top five firms in the accounting business. In 2001, AA&C reported over $9 billion in sales. Although they were such a huge corporate entity, being a publicly traded company made them not only accountable to the SEC, but also the public shareholders for their unethical actions. After the SEC conducted a thorough investigation, the court found Anderson management guilty of intent to cause employees to be deceitful about their business practices and to shred documents that were needed in a future investigation (Find Law, 2009). This finding shed a new light on how vulnerable an accounting firm can become when ethics are disregarded in management decisions. Various business groups were concerned that the prosecution of this accounting firm could set the stage for a number of investigations with all accounting firms. Arthur Andersen was reduced from 28,000 employees to about 200 employees as a result of the court's ruling (Flood, 2009). Three factors affecting business planning are the collection of existing information on current competitors, rebuilding public trust after the charges of unethical business practices have been brought out into the open, and the prevention of future actions by the company that would allow the public trust to be affected and the company to be subject to legal punishment. The new rules mandate that audit papers must be maintained for five to seven years. It also became against the law to destroy or alter any document that would be needed for an investigation, and provided for penalties of up to 20 years imprisonment if found guilty of doing so (Find Law, 2009). The introduction of the Sarbanes-Oxley Act led to more financial transparency. It outlined certain guidelines which must be adhered to such as reporting timelines, changes in responsibility of the audit committees. For the SEC and the public to be able to look in and evaluate the actions of these accounting companies, an increased trust should develop making way for more accurate investment and capital building processes. In conclusion, public corporations, financial institutions and accounting firms must become more responsible and honest in their practices. Sarbanes-Oxley is one of the most important pieces of accounting related legislation. If the U.S. is to continue to be marketable and expect to seek investment capital, financial transparency will continue to be an important goal (Kulzick 2004).

Just because someone is a leader does not necessarily mean that they are a good manager, but they can be both and that totally depends on the individual. One of the important attributes of a good leader is the ability to enact change in a business without getting too involved with the intricacies of the daily operations of the company. While being a manager, individuals will often times have the opportunity to hone their leadership abilities, but that is not always the case. A managers job requires them to be able to plan and stay within the budget projections, as compared to a leader's focus being primarily creating a vision and keeping people focused on the big picture.

Someone who is a manager can be effective even if they do not possess the ability to be a great leader. Managers run the day-to-day activities of the organization, making sure goals are met, personnel are where they are supposed to be, deadlines are not crossed without sufficient production parameters being addressed, etc. Leaders have the ability to project future achievements and keep the organization "alive" with new innovative techniques and they focus more on the long term goals and effects. Many managers are too concerned about the interaction with the workforce and they have to be political in their dealings with the employees, whereas leadership may have to make decisions that go against the grain at the time but hopefully those decisions are what is best for the company as a whole.

Both managers and leaders are vital to the success of any organization. While it may seem that a manager's job is monotonous and just a way for the leaders of the company to have their tasks fulfilled, a leader must take into account the nature of the business and how businesses operate on a grand scale. The book stated that there will be no business if it does not have a vision in place, and that is where a leader differs from a manager. Through research, development, innovation and intelligence gathering, a leader is able to be more aware of how outside influences are affecting their particular business.

Globalization has changed the effectiveness of management in several ways. At first, the term globalization seems to affect the way businesses think in terms of profitability, availability of products and resources, and legal aspects in dealing with foreign entities. The internet has played an important role in expansion and introduction of smaller businesses by allowing them access to resources, and by giving them a platform by which to market their goods and services to a broader consumer base. As technology advances, businesses are able to utilize the newest innovations in communication, research and development techniques, and delivery systems to accomplish their goals.

The idea of globalization is not entirely a new concept. Rulers, Kings, and self-appointed conquerors throughout the course of history have laid claim to land, assets and capital in an attempt for global domination and control of natural resources. I don't mean that every business seeks this achievement in their course of trying to turn a profit, but metaphorically speaking, globalization has been a part of the human psyche for thousands of years. As far as a leader optimizing their potential in different countries, I suppose that depends on the education level, ethical decision making ability, and moral values of the individual leader.

I would theorize that a leader should possess the ability to think outside the box in order to be most effective on a global scale. Things that would work in one country may be useless in another country. Take for instance marketing computer games in the United States versus a very poor third world country. In the U.S., many young children and adults enjoy playing video games as their pastime, but in a poor country where survival depends on the basic human needs such as food, water and shelter, they may not purchase such items of leisure, as they may be more likely to be focused on the purchase of shelf-stable food, clean bottled drinking water, or medical supplies. A good business leader would be able to predict marketing's effectiveness in such situations and act accordingly. The qualities of a leader will no doubt improve with each instance of them making tough decisions in order to keep their companies on a level of competition with both foreign and domestic businesses.

Organizing

Carolyn Lamm is the current President of the American Bar Association until 2010. Next year there will be a convention, where a new president will take her place, unless she holds her office for another term. She was born in Buffalo, New York and works in Washington, D.C., as a partner with White and Case, and was recently named one of the most influential women in America according to the National Law Journal (2007). Their diversification shows growth in leadership and ensures all people are represented by organizations concerning the legal profession.

Knowledge is paramount to the American Bar Association. Without a constant approach to tough issues and a gathering of resources, past cases and opinions, and a staff of leaders ready to assist in decisions and analysis, this organization could not be as useful to the law profession as it currently is. The ABA offers a wide variety of books on laws, regulations and other related topics. For instance, books on risk management and survival tools for laws firms are available. Case studies and topics on how the digital age of technology has affected modern law practices are also available (Davis and Jarvis 2007). To add to the knowledge base, the ABA has created an Information Security Committee to focus on the availability of new information, assuring that confidentiality remains secure, and assisting with the analysis of business and legal problems. With the increased use of the internet to contact clients and send data from one place to the next, an increase in cyber-security is relevant on keeping computer infrastructures safe from potential hackers. The ISC continues to provide management and service so the public will have the utmost confidence in the law firms in which they hire (Euromoney Institutional Investor PLC. 1999). Technology has played an important role in the practice of law. One of the largest assets to a law firm can be their computers and software, which cuts down on the time spent in travel and on site doing research. According to the Legal Technology Survey report, almost one third of the law firms in the United States have no means of keeping up with the technological advances due to budget constraints. Without this new technology, man-hours are spent on tedious research in libraries and courthouses, yet a number of lawyers who prefer it to be that way (Conner 2006).

The ABA offers resources and guidelines on how to manage a law firm effectively. They produce a magazine, Law Practice Management, which covers how to be profitable in a law practice and how to continue to build leadership skills. This publication also covers billable hours and how to maintain client service at optimum levels. The ABA is adamant on portraying their mission which is to serve their members and public equally, and the defense of liberty while delivering justice by means of legal professionals. The ABA goals are specifically defined as serving their members, improving the profession of law, eliminating bias, enhancing diversity, and to advance the rule of law in terms of accountability of government officials ((1) American Bar Association 2009).

As an organization, The American Bar Association realizes that independent courts are vital to the success of the law. When courts become overloaded and subject to political pressure from underlying powers that are not always apparent to the public, the ABA is determined to bring these issues up and try to reach a solution that best fits the role of justice. During dispute resolution, organizations like the ABA act as a third party for oversight purposes to ensure favoritism and bias are eliminated of decreased to a minimum ((2) American Bar Association 2009).

The ABA has optimized the use of organizational resources in terms of efficiency and effectiveness since its beginning. At nuclear power plants, control measures are required by the regulatory agency to ensure non-biased oversight and to make sure regulations, policies, and procedures are strictly followed. There are groups of QA (Quality Assurance) personnel and supervisors for Emergency Planning and other departments who have the responsibility to see that these controls are administered and that employees and contractors stay within compliance parameters. Since these controls are mandated by the Federal Government, the NRC (Nuclear Regulatory Commission) has the oversight authority over the plant and the leaders and managers who have been tasked with such duties. As a control measure, periodic and random inspections are conducted on all nuclear facilities in the United States. The controlling function of management may have negative connotations due to the human behavior element. There is a time of adjustment when control measures are put into place, and these measures can even result in dysfunctional behavior. Managers must take this into consideration and try to limit the resistance that may be felt by the workforce. When employees start resisting a new change, managers can use those employees who will comply to encourage the other employees that it is a good idea, and important for the success of the organization. The three factors managers should be aware of are rigid bureaucratic behavior, tactical behavior, and resistance. By using these behavioral assessments, a manager can effectively evaluate the resistance and acceptance and plan accordingly when they are involved in decision making. The control function of management is evolving in several ways. By providing adequate information and effectively communicating their proposals and by ensuring that the plans are accepted by employees, plans have a far greater chance of becoming reality. Resistance experienced by employees has a direct correlation to whether or not they accept the new management methods. When conditions change and some deviation from the plan is to be expected, employees should be able to voice their concerns without fear of reprimand; after all, it is the company that will profit from his communication as an end result. Controls are a necessary function of management to ensure the corporation, business, or organizations remains able to make a profit. Market controls are also used in regulating employees and company's performance.

One of the many types of control in business is bureaucratic control. This type of control comes from authority as it is designated in the organizational chart. As a person is elevated into higher echelons of managements, control measures will change accordingly. The drawback to an organization keeping too tight of control over their processes increases the likelihood of rigidity and leaves little room for change and growth. Managers have found ways to make corrections and adjustments to the bureaucracy that will allow their policies to be flexible and comparable to other types of control. One way is to allow feedback from the employee, and then implementing changes to policies as the need arises.

Another type of control is through regulative or market control. Market controls are set into place to adjust pricing to the consumer based on supply and demand. During holiday's seasons, limitations on certain items will indeed drive the price up as a result of scarcity. Regulative control begins with a company's standard method of operating, which some have deemed it to be outdated and having need for revamping. Organizations have been able to stretch the limitations of regulatory constraints in the past few years, making room for alliances with their competitors and allowing more flexibility in the global marketplace.

With the employees having more control over their own work output and being placed in supervisory roles, certain control measures are being adjusted to allow management more freedom to focus on the vision and the mission of the organization, and allowing the employees to have more responsibility at their level. My company provides us with a list of human performance topics to integrate into our pre-job briefings. One such topic is self-checking and another one is procedure adherence. These topics are explained to the employees prior to going on shift so they will be aware of them as control measures.

Chapter 10

Management and Leadership

Judicature is defined as the administering of justice, jurisdiction, and that which involves judges or courts collectively. Collectiveness is the key when it comes to the American Judicature Society. They are nearing 100 years of service to the legal community and the judicial system by providing answers to the tough questions in ethical professionalism and consistency in the court system. The American Judicature Society was founded on April 5, 1913 in Chicago, Illinois by Herbert Lincoln Harley, and is now headquartered in Des Moines, Iowa in The Opperman Center at Drake University. Harley, a progressive journalist who started off as a lawyer, had become dissatisfied with the old ways of the court system and how inconsistent the administration of justice was in America. After being inspired by a speech which condemned the current court leadership, he sought adequate funding to start his organization. The AJS is a nonpartisan (not connected with any single political party) organization of individuals in the legal profession that seeks to enhance the justice system and improve on those areas which have slowed down its progress. This allowed the court systems to remain focused on the correct and ethical administration of justice. It took over a dozen years for the ALS to become moderately influential in the judicial system, at which time they began publishing letters on the problems facing the system, and proposed plans to correct the errors. They drafted a model for the rules of civil procedure to provide consistency in the court systems to avoid favoritism, and they provided ideas and suggestions on how efficiency can be a large part of the court system. Carole Wagner Vallianos is the current president of the AJS. The reformation of the justice system was one of the goals of the AJS in joint cooperation with the Joint Committee for the Effective Administration of Justice. Among these reforms were items of interest such as judicial selection processes and judicial tenure, and the creation of a more unified state court system. The ALJ enjoyed increased membership over the years, and the leadership felt an overall expansion in their control over the organizations affairs. In 1974, Frederick D. Lewis became the volunteer leader of the AJS, lasting only two years due to an inadequate and problem filled administration. In 1982, the AJS was forced to pay back taxes on insurance policies they had been making available to their members, and it almost destroyed them financially. Volunteer leadership and the help of George H. Williams and others are credited for bringing the AJS back into normal operation (Belknap 2002). This goes to show that even an organization with the best intentions in mind can fall prey to scandal if the correct control measures are not strictly adhered to and in place. In this case, controls were not implemented or adhered to properly, and the management team had to take the necessary steps to correct the situation. (Bateman and Snell 2009).

One of the primary focuses of the AJS is to provide integrity, and to allow the American public to be aware of how the court system can benefit them in their lives, or when called upon for jury duty. Jury duty is not to be taken lightly, and the correct dispensing of justice is vital to the outcome of a verdict. Certain control measures are set in place such as confidentiality in selection and gag orders, or a court order to remain quiet about certain aspects of the case. The AJS, being a nonpartisan organization, can address tough issues without any alliances to certain political pressure of parties. They have a board of directors and other volunteer principles who have taken a leadership role in the oversight of the courts and on tough legal issues. The leadership that they have shown will enable the lawyers and judges to act according to principles of ethics and to not be concerned with political downfall due to the tough decision they must make on a daily basis. The administration of justice deals primarily with leadership decisions as compared to management decision making which can take place in the individual law firms or courts systems with personnel management (American Judicature Society, 2009).

Organizational managers have a responsibility in maintaining effective organizations and promoting healthy and creative cultures for their respective organizations. They can accomplish this by initiating change when it becomes necessary and appropriate and staying proactive in the processes which make a company competitive and marketable. Different individuals have shown leadership abilities that far exceed that which has been asked of them. Vallianos, the current AJS president, has an extensive background in non-partisan and nonprofit organizational management, and has a background in civil law (American Judicature Society 2009). According to Palm Beach Daily Business Review 2009, the AJS recognized former United States Attorney General Janet Reno as the recipient of their prestigious

Justice Award for her contributions to the American Justice System. She was the first woman to hold the office of attorney general and served in that position the longest. Mrs. Reno served the Clinton Administration for eight years until 2001. As a leader, Janet Reno has worked with various organizations in dealing with the proper administration of criminal justice since her retirement. The strategic plan put into place by the American Judicature Society is projected to be functional for up to five years. Based on their mission to insure fairness in the system of justice, the AJS seeks to promote qualified people to hold such offices. The AJS has also created a Law Firm Benefactor Program which supports the continued pursuit of judicial related work. Part of the organization's way of providing the public with as much information as possible is by publishing Judicature, which is an entity which allows for facts and opinions to surface. Those readers who wish to contribute can submit articles to the forum which is published every two months (American Judicature Society 2009). This is an example of clan control where the interpersonal processes of the organization can be shared and realized throughout the organization. Members of the AJS can share their common goals and interests by submitting their work to these forums, and other members can implement the new ideas and make adjustments to their own strategies. (Bateman and Snell 2009).

Management has been affected by a globalizing economy, and with trade routes being opened and reinforced across transnational borders. To address these issues, the various chapters of the AJS have stayed active in their role of oversight in campaign financing control, seeking a more independent judiciary, and providing more information to voters. According to Bateman and Snell (2009), one of the signs that an organization is in trouble is a lack of agreed upon standards.

Wechsler (2007) stated that the AJS has been on the forefront of minimizing how much political pressure can affect the judiciary. In the marketplace, controls are implemented to raise or lower prices in accordance with contributing factors. Sometimes these controls are adjusted in response to political entities working behind the scenes to drive a price in a certain direction to fill a need in some other area. The ALS seeks to bring this out into the public's arena, and reduce the chance that the economy could be adversely affected by this type of motivation and tampering. In addition, a merit plan has been introduced in 32 states for the ethical and non-biased selection of judges. Judges make law by decisions made in their cases which set precedent. If these judges act unethically, even the economy can be affected. A unified court system has been adopted by most courts in most states, and the AJS can at least take partial credit for this accomplishment. (Wechsler, 2007).

One method of insuring that managers and leaders continue to maintain a healthy organizational culture is by ensuring the jury pool is not corrupted. One of the primary focuses of the AJS is to act upon discrepancies in ethics and conduct in the criminal justice system. According to Indiana Courts (2006), "Today's [juror] list includes more than 99% of eligible jurors," compared to only 60%-80% in previous years. This achievement by the Indiana Court System won them praise and a special merit citation for their continued efforts to improve the jury selection process, and for implementing their "Jury Pool Project." This is an example of a bureaucratic control process where the organization can monitor progress. (Bateman and Snell). By increasing the public understanding of the American Justice system, and its enigmatic operations and language, the organization stays involved on several levels. The AJS has a tracking system which allows for direct interpretation and data collection of minorities and women and their role in the judicial process. For years, women and minorities had no voice in the legal field and struggle to reach a level of appointment due to under-representation. The National Center for State Courts (1998) Web site illustrates how studies on ethnic diversity on the bench have contributed to courts receiving and propagating merit plans, and through these merit plans, African Americans and women are more easily able to achieve an appointment to a judicial office. This concept is an example of a control method. By allowing business to operate as usual, the "good ole boy" mentality would persist, and minorities and those of lower socioeconomic backgrounds could suffer the inadequacy of lower ranking jobs and positions. To maintain a health system in the legal and judicial forums, a keen awareness of globalization and its affect on business matters must be maintained. Another way globalization has affected the legal community is by the increased need for lawyers who study international law and policies as companies expand to reach forgotten corners of the globe. In conclusion, the American Judicature Society has continued their pursuit of fairness and openness in the American Judicial System. With more than 5,000 current members and volunteers, the AJS remains a strong, viable and influential organization assisting the court system and those who practice law. They are essentially a control measure set in place to ensure the administration of justice remains consistent throughout the court system, and concerns can be addressed accordingly. Their diverse collection of attorneys and legal professionals make them a valuable asset in providing insight and scientific based ways of ensuring equitable outcomes in their approach to ethical problem solving (American Judicature Society 2009). By comparing their innovations and performance to the established standards of conduct, they display an example of control measures, and continue to pursue excellence in operation (Bateman and Snell 2009).

I can see where using brainstorming can enhance the flow of ideas and have an effect on the final decision, as well as framing the problem. I would say that it is just as important to have a session with critical thinkers so we don't end up with just a storm, and no positive use of the brain. Everything we do in the business world involves some risk. As managers and supervisors, we need to be proactive in identifying risks, and we should also take steps in trying to lower the chances of a risk occurring, although at times it will be unavoidable. Our teams should include managers who have a responsibility for implementing change and addressing risks, and those who can give us advice from previous experience in dealing with these issues. In order for us to be able to tell our colleagues and managers what a problem is we can use the persuasive communication template. In this template, we can set our objectives, discover the background of the issue, determine the cost benefit and scope of the decision, and provide our solution based on our decision and a plan to implement it (Langdon, 2001). Convergent thinking is when information is available to a decision-maker, and their decision tends to come together at a collective centralized point. This type of thinking is generally seen when managers align themselves after a meeting. Managers can different opinions during the meeting but there is usually one final decision at the conclusion of that meeting. In contrast, divergent thinking is when decision-makers move in different directions, essentially branching off with multiple problem solving approaches (Cronbach, 1963). This can be important in international and culturally diverse operations where the old way of doing business does not meet the current organizational model for successful business decisions. "Thinking is a continual process of going places, of changing knowledge and finding oneself in a new 'state of mind." (Schroyens, 2005, p. 163). The latter statement provides an explanation and a foundation for trenchant cognition, albeit a theoretical one. Nielsen, Pickett, and Simonton (2008) stated that critical thinking may need to be explored to a greater length when conducting research, as compared to creative thinking in the artistic world. Critical thinking develops over time when applied to everyday scenarios. In cases of bad decision making and unethical practices, the possibility of a lack of critical thinking must be present.

Weighing the factual information, projecting that decisions impact on a company or corporation, and making decisions based on moral and ethical principles will eliminate the detrimental effects of decision making void of criticism. To reiterate the methods involved with divergent thinking, an abundant amount of possibilities will surface to be at the disposal of the decision-maker. It is not a one-sided viewpoint, and divergent thinking can produce astounding results if implemented properly. The path for critical thinkers is paved with past experiences, feedback from operational personnel, and an innate ability to forecast where a good or bad decision may lead them forward into the future.

Making decisions requires several levels of integrated pieces of information. When we think critically, we are utilizing these pieces to construct a response that will achieve a desired goal. That goal may be in the form of a response during a debate, completing a task at work or a decision to stay at home and study instead of going out on a Saturday night with friends. Regardless of the circumstance, we think critically when we reach inside of ourselves for an answer that may not be immediately apparent. Our decisions are based upon knowledge that we have acquired from past events, facts that are being presented at the given moment, our perception of the ramifications of our final decision and how it will affect the outcome, and they can even be affected by outside influences and stimuli (such as other people's opinions and views of our society).

It is my opinion that critical thinking is beneficial to the growth and development of leaders, managers and students in that thought processes inherently mold us into who we are as individuals. As we strive to complete our daily work and align ourselves with what is beneficial and profitable for our families and co-workers, we must think critically to ensure those decisions are contributing to a positive and moral outcome. If we choose to make rash decisions based on fatuous assumptions, and if we agree to cheat ourselves of the intellectual guidance which our own consciousness provides us, we only restrict ourselves to the chains which bind our talents.

There have been times in my own life where I have made decisions which seemed correct at the time, but later turned out to be detrimental to my situation. Perhaps if I had thought critically about the end result, or if I had chosen to allow myself the freedom of thought instead of the primal urge to rely on instinct, the path where I ended up would have been more satisfying. I am still learning how not to be my own worst enemy. Each lesson that I learn which includes how to think critically is cataloged in an area of my brain where I believe it will someday be put to good use in helping me determine the correct course of action, and help my decision-making process in the future.

At the beginning, identifying the cause of the problem can take some time to accurately gather all needed information. This may involve a root-cause analysis to discover what information can substantiate the critical components necessary to deliver a sound decision. Next, by framing the alternatives, the decision maker is provided with a path in which to resolve different methods into elements. Evaluating the impacts of those alternatives will ensure all directives have been met and any new idea can be incorporated in the decision to which fact and practicality can be utilized. Finally the individual is at the point of actually making the decision. At this point, information has been evaluated, and even though evaluating the impact of the decision is part of the last step in the model, a forward thinker will anticipate the consequences of their actions. These steps cover most of what is needed in order to make critical decision.

To recapitulate how indispensible the decision making process can be, you must be aware of how immoral and detrimental resolutions can adversely impact society, and how bad decision making processes affect the individuals in our companies and communities. By following a model that explains how to effectively deliver a sound decision based on good judgment, and by moving forward by seeking out the truths in every situation, we will begin to see the difference that can be made by our actions.

Chapter 11

Critical Thinking Application

In the global economy, business owners and managers must think critically about their decision making processes and how their businesses and the other businesses they deal with are affected. A multifaceted approach is required due to the expansion of the marketplace and the amount of variables that companies encounter. If managers are to be respected for their decisions they must think critically about the outcomes of those decisions by incorporating all necessary information and techniques that they have used in prior situations.

Critical thinking is the process of solving problems while taking a look at all available options and information related to that problem and arriving at the best possible solution. With each given scenario, a group of possible solutions presents itself, leaving the decision maker responsible for evaluating all options. Thinking critically has become more important in the business environment due to the advancement in technology and the operation of businesses in the global marketplace. Managers will need to take into account the time that is required for their employees to adjust to any new decisions and the managers must take time to think critically about the process in regard to how their decisions affect their organizations as a whole.

To think critically, managers must take into consideration the two types of critical thinking. Divergent thinking involves analyzing a given problem and arriving at various options or solutions which would best serve the decision-making process. In contrast, convergent thinking involves evaluating all given information and formulating only one solution. Both methods can be valuable when making decisions (Cronbach 1963). Critical thinking allows a manager to arrive at vital decisions with the assurance that all angles were covered and all possible scenarios were addressed. The benefit of critical thinking would have to be an increase in the amount of good, solid decisions which eliminate mistakes and potential time-wasting reorganizing sessions.

One critical thinking skill is being able to find the critical issues in certain complex situations. The answers may not always be available so research may have to be conducted to ensure any regulation or policy that is involved is not violated. When dealing with problem solving, finding the actual cause for what is wrong, and making the best possible choice in an appropriate amount of time is important. Managers must identify and respond to various potential threats and opportunities and act accordingly. These critical thinking skills can be taught by management, but they can also be learned through experience and dedication to doing the right thing (Pascarella 1997).

I have been able to use critical thinking at my job. During a refueling outage, an increase in staffing is needed and more responsibility gets placed upon our organization. Timetable limits must be adhered to, and certain areas of the plant require additional personnel to be in place for monitoring purposes. My job has consisted of scheduling those personnel and ensuring that all requirements have been met, and all goals have been achieved. During plant emergencies, it takes quite a bit of coordination to get any injured personnel out of the protected area and headed to the nearby medical facility. Our managers and supervisors are constantly training on various weapons and tactical response scenarios in order to protect the plant and the public from a disaster. Training involves thinking critically about what we are defending against and constantly updating our knowledge base on matters of homeland security. I am required to speak in generalities only due to the sensitive nature of my job, and to ensure safeguards information is protected. In summary, we can realize that most of our behavior involves some type of problem solving and critical thinking. When we learn to look around at possible connections of pieces of information, we realize that our decisions can be based on factual principles. Being aware that two different people can arrive at two different solutions given the same exact facts shows us that the decision making process is subjective. The effective manager will only accept checked and verified conclusions and will keep their thinking free from emotional distractions. Our decisions affect our organizations on many levels including the way our employees view our effectiveness. We must continue to seek out new methods of critical thinking and learn how to apply that thinking to real life situations. I still would have to say that making and implementing the decision would help me with my style of decision-making. Making tough decisions has been a work in progress for me, and I try to learn from those who I respect as good and effective leaders. Information can be confusing especially in a stressful situation, and there have been times when I have made the wrong decisions based on my feelings or assumptions instead of good data. One time at the plant, I dispatched personnel to an emergency event but during the process, I failed to tell them to get the employee's badge numbers who would be leaving the plant through the gate and not the turnstiles. The next day when those employees tried to reenter the plant, they were locked out and had to wait until the alarm station could resolve the matter. This could have been avoided if I had taken a little extra time and passed on the needed information. At the time, I made the decision to handle the emergency as quickly as possible without looking ahead at any possible future problems that could arise. Decisions reflect solutions to problems —we need to address the issues first. Making decisions requires an evaluation of alternative options against selection criteria. Not all selection criteria will be equally important or influential in making the choice. The current choice or status quo should always be considered to ensure that performance will improve as the result of the decision. The current choice or status quo will always be tested by an alternative option. The decision-makers will never leave the point of the decision without thinking about the steps necessary to implement the decision successfully. These principles will help me in making and effective decision by providing an outline or a set of guidelines to direct the flow of information and ideas and help me to respond accordingly. By addressing the issues first, I will be able to clearly see what it is I am trying to work on and not go about making my decision half-heartedly. I will need to do an evaluation to see if there is a better way to approach the decision or a better way of solving it, and to not be afraid of using a different method. Some things that seem important to my decision may need to be discarded prior to reaching my result, because some information may not be as important. The existing state of affairs may need to be improved and will definitely need to be tested to ensure performance. Last, I will need to think about my decision and the steps I took to arrive at my conclusion. I can see these principles helping me at my current job. I can take a little extra time to implement them into my decision-making process in order to become a more effective supervisor. It seems that I have already used some of them without even being aware of what they were, perhaps it was just good common sense. I believe that creating a business case template will help streamline business processes, maximize the utilization of available staff and contribute to service enhancement. Business cases can be developed to support funding requests for next year's budget, and they need to explain who is going to use the case, when they need it, which existing plans or future plans will the case contribute to and other essential planning criteria. At a minimum, the business case should consist of two alternative means of carrying out the proposal, including an executive summary. Building a business case would help me in my personal life right now as opposed to a business; perhaps in my workplace also. I could identify problems that I am facing now such as time constraints due to work and school, and trying to juggle quality time with my family. It would also help me to write down alternative plans if the ones that I am currently working on don't work out exactly like I want them to. At my place of work, it could help me to prioritize job tasks and evaluations that I have to write for employees.

In the future, I plan on working for myself, but not until I graduate from Law School. At this time, I will need to have a good working knowledge of running a business and management the workforce, or even if it is just me for a few years, I will need to project budgets and recognize market trends and budgets. A business case could help me in financial models and cash flow projections, and in managing risks and having a contingency checklist. I believe it is important to avoid starting from a weak premise, which is the first trap. This kind of judgment trap involves passing judgment without having all of the correct information. A weak premise can be formed from a minor premise, which is one-third of a syllogism. A minor premise is when you make a factual assertion about a person or group, usually considered a statement of fact, but in the case of a weak premise, all facts are not clear or apparent. When a judgment is "anchored," the person making the judgment starts with a premise that they alone believe to be true. If they don't have the correct information about their decision, their premise will be weak, and their argument will have no substantive grounds. In legal arguments, a minor premise is usually referred to as a *statement of fact.* This is why I chose this judgment trap, because I want to avoid weak arguments when I get into law school. According to our reading, decisions are often based upon people wanting a clone of themselves (while hiring employees), instead of picking the right person to fill the job. Their premise is weak when they stereotype employees based on previously accepted norms, when they don't properly evaluate the new employee to see their strengths and education. This can lead to a loss of potentiality for the company, in that the new employee may be the best person for the job, despite the hiring individual's bias or lack of information about that potential employee. To effectively compile a conclusion, pass judgment, or arrive at a sensible decision, the conclusion may need to consist of tying the minor premise (particular statement) together with a major premise (general statement that is something we know to be true and accepted by most people). I believe it is necessary to gather all relevant facts on a situation before passing judgment, because during moot (debate) sessions, a weak premise can destroy the foundation of a good argument, regardless of the speakers' intent.

Last year, I contemplated buying a local business in the town where I live. I called the owner to let him know that I would be there to meet with him at 7:45am. I informed him that if he would in fact be there, a return phone call was not necessary, but if he couldn't make it, to please call me. I arrived at the business at 7:40am, called him at 7:45am, and left a message. 7:50am, he called and informed me that he would not be able to make it due to unlocking a house for another contractor, so he rescheduled for 9:30am later today. At 8:42am, he called and cancelled our appointment, and he asked if tomorrow would work for appointment, I informed him that I had to be in school in Arlington and would not be able to make it, not to mention the fact that I had to arrange a babysitter while we were supposed to meet today. I never heard back from the guy after that day. I felt that this was rude behavior from someone who actually wanted to sell his business, so it was probably best that it ended up this way. I have known managers at other previous jobs who acted in this manner. They would schedule things and then either not show up or cancel on you at the last moment. This shows improper planning and I don't want to be that way. I remembered the above scenario in detail because I put it into my journal of unusual events. I record so much information in that journal, and in a way, that is like my business reference material for the future. By recording situations, I can go back and review them and learn from them.

Thoreau (1995) stated, "But lo! Men have become the tools of their tools" (p. 24). Henry David Thoreau was a naturalist who died in 1862, but even then was able to express to an audience how important simplicity was, and the appreciation of simpler things. Materialism has become a way of life for many Americans, and it is a sad state of affairs. I suppose growing up economically challenged, I feel the need to respond to this post, but I do not want to be misunderstood as someone who feels a sense of entitlement. Inflation in this country has been elevated so high that now it is necessary for both parents to work and support the family, just to make a living wage. Who does this leave to raise the children; these children are our posterity and it is vital that we get a grip on our current condition before the end no longer satisfies the means. When

Thoreau decided to go off and live in the woods in Massachusetts, it was at that time that he was able to do a self-evaluation of all that humans held important, vital for their existence, and frivolous. Perhaps it is time that we do the same. Organizations are realizing that they are not isolated, and leaders of these organizations are experiencing the value of healthy communities who seek to do the right thing. Knowing too well that ethical responsibility goes way beyond our immediate surroundings, leaders as well as workers must take appropriate steps to implement ethics into their daily operational tasks.

When people start to understand the importance of ethics, that is right and wrong behavior and how it relates to their specific situation, they begin to lay down the ground rules that will dictate their future actions. As people begin to change their habits or to reinforce old standards that were based on morality and ethical representation, they begin to cope with problems with a new perspective, and thus clear the conscious of the emotional baggage attached to committing acts of unethical proportions (Trevino & Nelson, 2004).

Personally, I deal with ethical decisions and situations which can affect employee morale and participation in the processes that are set in place by our management. A former place of employment encouraged honesty and integrity and a safe culture where problems, complaints and concerns can be addressed without fear of retaliation. There was a situation about two years ago where an upper level manager was harassing female subordinates. Apparently, this had been going on for quite some time. The employees within my organization, as a cohesive group, decided to take action and alert the district human resource manager about the allegations.

A thorough investigation was conducted, but there was not enough substantive evidence against the individual at the time. About a year later, that same individual was involved in another serious but unrelated incident. The previous investigation laid the groundwork for a pattern of behavior, so the new investigation was taken even more seriously. Subsequently, the individual is no longer with our company. I believe that the group ethical process was utilized. The group of employees handled the matter in accordance with our policies and procedures and the situation was documented. If no one had been willing to report this individual's wrong behavior, they may still be with the company.

I intend to learn valuable information and techniques that will assist me in the ethical practice of law in the future. To me, a strong moral and ethical background is essential in the interpretation of facts and the implementation of processes in our daily lives and in our business practices. In the past, ethical dilemmas have risen to the forefront of the news when higher echelons of management chose to do the wrong thing, notwithstanding an understanding of the way they should have conducted their business practices. I want to be an ethically responsible attorney. Reputation can make or break you when you are an individual practitioner, and an ethical approach to business is essential for growth and success. I am also interested in the way other people feel about ethics. If I am the only one concerned about right and wrong, it would be hard to maintain such a standard during due process. For instance, if I am retained as council to defend someone who I believe to be innocent but find out later that they withheld pertinent information from me as a result of deception, I still have an ethical responsibility to tell the truth, and their case may be affected. Perhaps in this class I will gain the tools necessary to deal with such a conflict. The way others view their lives and conduct has a direct influence on how I may perceive the importance of doing the right thing. Regardless, I plan on doing the right thing while providing a positive image; I will be an advocate for the moral and ethical high ground.

Personal Values Development

"Providing for honest things, not only in the sight of the Lord, but also in the sight of men" (Holy Bible: King James Version, 1989; II Corinthians 8:21). I believe in the importance of being truthful and doing what is right, even during those times when ethical decisions seem difficult to make. At times, I have been in the company of "managers" who had no reason in holding that position. They lacked management training, morals, ethics and good common sense. Ethics is a branch of philosophy defined as the study of what constitutes right or wrong behavior (Clarkson, Miller, Jentz & Cross, 2009).

My grandfather taught him to be honest and fair and to consider others when making decisions. I lived in nine different houses and mobile homes during my childhood, and at times I have a wandering gypsy mentality that seeks to let me release the constraints of modern day commitments that seem too concrete. This constant motion, the constant moving on average of every two years seemed to forge me into a man who is rarely able to feed my insatiable appetite for more than just the status quo. My ethics are simply put into one paragraph. I believe that there may be forces beyond my control, which at times seek to limit my success. An individual must be morally strong enough to combat these external forces to reach the self-enlightenment that they wish to obtain. The right thing is always the best thing, and that is the path that

I have chosen for my life. As previously mentioned, the sources for my ethical platform are the good influence that I experienced from my grandfather, and the Biblical teachings that I struggled with during my youth. According to Trevino & Nelson (2004), "Good character alone simply doesn't prepare people for the special ethical problems they are likely to face in their jobs or professions," (Trevino & Nelson, 2004. p. 11). I believe the aforementioned is a true statement, and an individual must also work hard at learning from their experiences to learn ethical awareness. You must also learn to adapt and realize that just because someone holds the title of manager that does not mean they actually know how to manage.

Responsibility does play an important role in the human ethical decision making processes. I just finished a book of four court cases. In one of the cases, a bank president found himself in an ethical dilemma. According to Black (1999), in 1988, Fred De La Mata was federally indicted on money laundering charges, as well as bribery. He was president of a large bank in Miami, Florida. Due to an unethical decision that he made to accept a large monetary gift from one of his best bank customers, it took over four years of legal pursuits to have his guilty verdict overturned. According to Roy Black, his defense attorney, Mr. De La Mata still has trouble being hired by any bank due to pressure from federal prosecutors who regularly inquire about those who try to offer him help and assistance in employment. It was alleged that he established a quid pro quo by accepting a gift in exchange for a guarantee of a home loan for a valued customer (Black, 1999). A quid pro quo is in laymen's terms "this for that." In taking a gift, a business owner can jeopardize their credibility because once accepted, the gift acts as a bargaining chip for future pay-offs, which is highly unethical. Business owners and corporate CEO's have to be especially concerned about ethical business practices. Black (1999) stated, "The guy on top of the pyramid makes the biggest target" (p. 252). Responsibility comes with positions of power. It was eventually found that the bank president was not guilty, but it cost him a lot of money in attorney fees and damage to his previously good reputation with all of the bad media publicity. This situation raised questions about Mr. De La Mata's virtue ethics, in that he was charged with violation of professional codes of responsibility as defined by the banking institution and how the community perceives gift giving (Trevino & Nelson 2004, p. 93). The Internet has opened up the proverbial "can of worms" when it comes to conflicts of interests and employee/employer expectations and behavior. "A conflict of interest occurs when your judgment or objectivity is compromised [usually judged by a third party]" (Nelson & Trevino 2004, p. 67). For instance, a company has strict policies regarding morality, sensitivity to certain ethnic groups, and overall respect for other employees and an employee is caught posting abusive language and pictures to Face book or some other social networking site. Once a comment or picture is posted to the Internet, it falls prey to public scrutiny and can cause the termination of employment for those who abuse the privilege. Businesses did not deal with these issues prior to the 1990's, and it seems that violators are being dealt with at an alarming rate. This type of behavior from an employee affects the global perspective of the company by shareholders and customers, and it may be damaging to sensitive individuals if the harassment is directed toward them. Third parties who may view unacceptable posting by employees could include but are not limited to competitors, customers, and government groups who look for certain types of language on the internet.

Managers can resolve conflicts in the workplace by applying a utilitarian approach. That is to say managers can identify several alternative methods to approach and solve problems and address those issues where the end result would be in the best interest of all who are involved. This may mean special meeting designed to iron out differences in opinion, or ways of doing business, or something as serious as alternative dispute resolution involving human resources and legal counsel. After all methods are exhausted, it may be in the company's and the stakeholder's best interest to terminate the employee's position with the company, depending on the pertinent issues (Trevino & Nelson 2004, p. 89).

There may also be times where it would be in the individual employee to quit a job where their ethical principles are being compromised by the actions of the company. The company and its management may be so determined to obtain a return on their investment and gain profits that they step over ethical thresholds. If this causes an employee to question their own behavior and actions at work, then for the sake of a clear conscience they should make the decision to work elsewhere. In contrast, it may be the individual who is compromising the company's expectation for ethical behavior of their employees, and in that case, a thorough investigation may be warranted, and the company may decide to release the employee and end the company-employee relationship.

On a personal level, a person's ethical standards are set in place when they are young and they have had their whole life up to this point to correct bad behavior, accept their ethics the way they are, and the opportunity for self improvement. At the professional level, managers and supervisors may be new to the role which they are currently holding, and some adjustment may be necessary for them to completely do their jobs at optimum performance. Managers are accountable for the entire human resource departments in their respective companies, and they act as role models for workers in their departments. In their (managers) personal lives, they are ethical at the micro level, in that their decisions may primarily be toward family, and household responsibilities.

Chapter 12

System of Inquiry

Henry Ford said, "The only real security that a man can have in this world is a reserve of knowledge, experience and ability." These are at least three attributes that Securitas employees and management possess. Starting at the very top of the organization, Securitas has been a leader in providing accurate information on security systems, diligent men and women to watch over owner-controlled areas, ethical implementation of problem-solving techniques and decision-making processes and they back it up with many years of experience. Codes of conducts, ethical systems and implementation and effect will all be determining factors in the Securitas system of ethical management. Leadership in the global economy requires that companies have a code of conduct or ethical behavior, and managers provide an ethical workplace for all employees (Securitas AB, n.d.).

General Information

Securitas is a versatile security company with many market interests. Over the years they have purchased several small security companies including Burns and Pinkerton. They operate in North America, and many other countries around the world. The company can address specific needs based on client requirements and can tailor make services to fulfill industry demands. Securitas provides investigation services, armed and unarmed guards, camera monitoring services, and consulting services for applicable clients. Securitas includes in their mission statement their ability to protect American homes, jobsites, and surrounding communities, while being able to make a reasonable profit. Their core values include integrity, vigilance, and helpfulness to their clients. Securitas management uses these tools to conduct their decision-making processes and guide their leadership in their profession (Securitas AB, n.d.).

Code of Conduct

The code of conduct requires all employees to exhibit respect and professionalism toward coworkers and clients. The code also encourages employees to adhere to the strong ethical philosophy that is paramount with the success of the company and its shareholders. Guidelines for minimum age requirements and wage limitations also can be found in this document. Securitas is a leader in staying within acceptable parameters of government regulations and industry standards (Securitas AB, n.d.). In the past, violations of this code have led to employment termination and investigations of all individuals involved.

Implementing a code of ethical conduct in a business is one of the most effective ways for that business to set the tone concerning behavior. According to Clarkson, Miller, Jentz, and Cross, (2009), a conduct code should allow employees to raise concerns and complaints to upper-level management without fear of reprimand. A well-written code will specify ethical behaviors that will be accepted at the workplace (p. 106).

Ethical System

Securitas uses a duty-based ethical approach in business decision-making (Nelson & Trevino, 2004, p. 91). They base their belief system on honesty and integrity to the client, and by demanding a high ethical standard of all employees. Their managers are taught to do the right thing and to pass that philosophy on to the officers in the field. The protection of property and lives is a daily responsibility for the officers who accept the various security related duties. These duties include camera observation of owner controlled areas, filling out security field reports, investigation of theft, accidents and suspicious persons and vehicles and protection against nuclear sabotage and theft of nuclear trade secrets and materials. Surrounding communities rely on the Securitas Company to provide security to ensure safety of all citizens. The safety of citizens is a top priority for Securitas leadership (Securitas AB, n.d.).

Code of Conduct Use and Implementation

Securitas management must learn to trust their employees so those employees will be able to work in unsupervised areas and maintain client trust. Securitas managers are required to comply with industry standards in ethical approaches to problem-solving and are taught to embrace and protect the diverse work culture that exists. Many Securitas managers started out as entry-level security officers. They have a working knowledge of how their officers and supervisors will react in a given situation. The Securitas board of directors meets at least six times annually and their work procedures are in accordance with the Swedish Companies Act as well as other applicable laws. In these meetings, they discuss corporate governance and the growth and health of the company, and that all executives are staying within acceptable guidelines. The Securitas website provides general information about its board of directors, but little about ethical governance. Most of the ethical conduct is found at the branch or site level. All companies are required to have a code of ethics and make their employees aware of that code (Securitas AB, n.d.).

Summary

The code of conduct currently used by Securitas Security Services Inc. provides a detailed account of their commitment to their clients, employees, leaders, and surrounding communities. With their duty-based ethical approach to problem-solving and ethical decision-making, Securitas demands professionalism of their employees and managers to ensure clients are taken care of and objectives are met. Responsibility plays an important role when protecting another's property of life. The code of conduct acts as a platform on which good ethics and responsible decisions can be based in the workplace and at home (Securitas AB, n.d.).

Using the utilitarian approach, we can stop to analyze our own actions and belief systems, and that of the company we work for and from there we can decide what is right. If the actions of the company are way off base from what we hold as personal values and ethics, we can either choose to leave the company, or we can take appropriate steps to try to change the workplace environment. Nothing is ever set in stone, so there is a chance that a proposal by us toward ethical behavior can be implemented into the company processes for future advancement of ethical standards (Nelson & Trevino, 2004, p. 90).

We had a situation at work where teasing and horseplay was getting out of hand. Apparently this had been going on for many years, and no one had addressed the issue. Once our new project manager came in a couple of years ago, he called a company meeting to address issues affecting performance and human behavior errors. He stated that he realized this was part of our culture and that in a way it helped strengthen our camaraderie and group cohesion, but it had to stop immediately. He didn't just tell us to stop the behavior; he took the time to tell us why. Horseplay can lead to someone getting hurt or injured on company property and the teasing could put the company at risk for a harassment claim. After an open group discussion which lasted for a long time, the employees saw that for the good of the company and the group as a while, the behavior would have to be modified. I believe this would be an example of how personal ethics van be changed to be in alignment with company ethics.

Chapter 13

Mind and Consciousness of Machines and Humans

Abstract

This essay will include a critique of John Searle's arguments on free will, Victor Frankl's examination of meaning and purpose in life, the differences between syntactic knowledge and semantic knowledge, the differences between the form and content of knowledge, and the concepts of mind, consciousness, and knowledge. The study and research of artificial intelligence and machines that one day may think independently will open new doors of opportunity in regard to the mind-machine problem.

Critique of John Searle's arguments

According to Searle (1984), "[human] brains cause minds, and minds have mental contents" (p. 39). The fact that a mind exists is a direct result of biological processes, and there is more going on inside the brain than mere computation. "There is more to having a mind than having formal or syntactical processes" (Searle, 1984, p. 31). The brain functions with all aspects of language, sight, and senses, respectfully. By inputting data or downloading these processes in a mechanical way, "The way that brains cause minds cannot be solely in virtue of a computer program" (Searle, 1984, p. 40). In terms of free will, Searle believes that humans experience free will by thinking about it. He explained, "Nothing we do is free in any philosophically interesting sense (Searle, 1984, p. 91) Libertarianism is a philosophical approach to try and explain what man wants in terms of freedom and individual liberty. He asks, "If libertarianism is true, as the thesis of free will, would we have to fundamentally change our belief systems" (Searle, 1984, p. 92)? "If we apply the lessons of causality and intentionality in regard to the human brain and its processes, shouldn't we be able to account for the brain's ability to cause minds?" (Searle, 1984, p. 22). Searle answered no to the question about inserting the right programming will lead to thinking (Searle, 1984, p. 36). Andrew Jones believes that a Divine Designer provided the human existence and their consciousness, allowing us to experience life according to our choices and interests. The exception, of course, occurs when other humans become over takers of a group, thus dominating their lives; that is not in the plan of that higher power, yet it is allowed to continue. Andrew believes that humans have free will. Free will is a natural right given to us. Every time a human makes a purchase and credit is used for payment, a computer monitors and tracks the transaction. This could be an invitation to the loss of free will and liberty. Andrew also believes that artificial intelligence research and development will provide the foundation upon which an artificial mind will operate. A machine with a mind can be an important asset to the scientific community.

Meaning and purpose in life

Victor Frankl endured the hardships and horrors of a German concentration camp in Auschwitz, Poland. During his imprisonment, he learned a great deal about the human condition, and the meaning and purpose of life. He stated, "A human being is a finite thing, and his freedom is restricted" (Frankl, 1984, p. 153). Freedom is restricted. Humans are only free from restraints in terms of psychological adaptation to stressful and unpleasant situations. We allow ourselves to go to a "happier" place to avoid the shock that prisoners have endured. Frankl initiated a form of psychiatry and named it "Logotherapy" (Frankl, 1984, p. 120).

Logotherapy is a way of interpreting psychological phenomenon by reducing it to its emotional origin (Freeman, Mahoney, Devito, Martin, 2004, p. 83). Existential frustration provides us with an understanding of existence (Frankl, 1984, p. 123). Frankl realized that the fact that humans can adapt to situations and bring happy events into their circle of misery. This would lead a researcher to believe that Frankl would see purpose and meaning to be specifically human traits, the exception would be if scientists could create a machine that could find its own purpose for existence and find meaningful actions to keep it occupied during times of depression and misery. The machine would have to succumb or circumvent a plethora of human or human-like emotions to accomplish this high-level response.

Attitudes may cause a difference in opinion, in that people will have different ideas of artificial intelligence and its role in our lives, and the fact that in the very near future, we may have to discuss these problems that had not existed in previous psychological experiments. Frankl believed that by maintaining a tragic optimism, humans could keep their purpose regarding life despite of tragic circumstances (Frankl, 1984, p. 161). In contrast, machines may conduct routine tasks without questioning their intended purpose. In the post-industrial age that we live in, it is extremely important for those of us who possess the natural knowledge of growing our own food and surviving during scarcity to pass this knowledge on to our posterity. The fact that the world seems to be moving at an increased pace on a day-to-day schedule impedes the time spent on what is beneficial for the human body and mind. Today, the average American school child could not possibly be able to explain what farm animal produces milk, and which one produces eggs. Andrew Jones believes that machines will have a purpose in helping us to grow crops and do meaningful tasks. These machines will eventually develop a consciousness, but it will not be for survival reasons, it will strictly be a matter of programming.

Syntactic knowledge and semantic knowledge

Dürsteler (2010), "syntactic knowledge is the information that needs to be memorized and maintained by a user in order to efficiently use a certain system (Syntactic Knowledge, para. 1). Computer programmers must have a certain amount of background knowledge in order to effectively write programs. (Dürsteler, 2010). Syntax is defined as the way in which terms are combined to form phrases and sentences. It is the branch of grammar dealing with phrases and sentences formation. Thirdly, it is the rules governing the construction of a machine language.

In contrast, semantics is the study or science of meaning in language forms, with regard to historical changes. It is also the study of the relationship between signs and symbols and what they represent to their interpreter. Searle stated, "In a word, the mind has more than syntax, it has semantics" (Searle, 1984, p. 31). He went on to explain how a computer, at this point, could not possess a mind because it lacks the semantic content of the human brain (Searle, 1984). Syntactic knowledge would include ones and zeros used by computers to communicate with each other. Humans communicate by visual cues in terms of body language interpretation, the five senses, and standard communication methods (writing, phone call, signals, etc.).

Computer language is sent and received without regard to feeling. Tone in communication is very important, as the person on the other end does not have the visual part of the conversation; only the text. Computer designers will have to tackle the issue of syntax versus semantic language as part of their artificial intelligence development processes. Semantics can pose a difficult problem when sending a text message. If the sender is in a hurry and doesn't provide enough background information for a request, the message can seem harsh and abrasive. Syntax is fast, in that many messages, documents, or photos can be sent through a USB port at rapid speed, without regard to interpretation at that point. Humans deal with semantics, in terms of justifying the communications they have sent. John Searle made the statement that computers will never have a mind. His analogy was that computers operate on syntax, and therefore lack the content of the human brain (Searle, 1984). Andrew believes computers will have a mind, and a scientist will find a way to add content to a machine's internal processes.

Differences between the form and content of knowledge

Formal knowledge is what is agreed upon and taught in the classroom by academics. Informal knowledge is usually past on through our families, learned through our experiences, or taught in churches and other community organizations. A difference between tacit and explicit knowledge is the former is knowledge that is not in our consciousness, and the latter is knowledge that is in our consciousness. Tacit knowledge does not need to be verbalized in our communication with others. It may have been a primal response and a survival instinct before standardized language was developed.

Searle used the analogy of a Chinese speaker and someone who was in a room receiving input, and arbitrarily sending out responses in Chinese. The person in the room did not possess the formal Chinese language or the content, he was just passing out predetermined cards written in the language to those on the outside (Searle, 1984). "Our attitudes to the possibility of consciousness in animals and machines are clouded in the doubts [of our limited knowledge] of molecular processes and the connection to our biology" (Zeman, 2002, p. 341).

Concepts of mind, consciousness, and knowledge

Mind is the center of thought, feeling, and intellect. It typically deals with memory, intention, and intellect, but its definition has not been agreed upon by psychologists (Chaplin, 1985). Consciousness is being aware. Knowledge is what is known or learned. Artificial intelligence is the science of computer intelligence, as defined. Intelligence is the ability to learn or solve problems, or news and information. Zeman (2002) stated, "Describing the function of the human brain and artificially implementing it is the 'ultimate goal' of work in the [field] of artificial intelligence (p. 322).

Similarities exist between machine intelligence and intelligence that human being possess. Mind, as we know it, is a biological process created by the human brain that allows us to know that we are asking questions about our very existence. Our minds allow us to process information, analyze that information and then make decisions based on our enormous store of facts, figures, and common knowledge. Machines do this by means of a central computer, which metaphorically acts much like the brain in terms of being the central part of the decision-making process. Computers do this by responding to input data, either from a sensor or computer programmer, and the brain does this by electro-chemical reactions and nerve endings. Andrew believes that certain elements in the field of AI will remain ambiguous. By completely removing all traces of skepticism to let the higher self flourish, humans will reach an altered state of consciousness that will allow them to reach the unexplained intelligence and deeper mysteries. All wisdom-seeking individuals want to achieve this state during their natural lives on Earth. I don't believe a consciousness can be taught. A consciousness is developed as we go through adolescence and into adult hood. Morals can be taught. I do believe that right and wrong behavior can be taught and instilled in a child at an early age. I would say that we become consciousness around age 3, but we really start to question the world, life and who we are around puberty. Before that, our parents or caretakers instruct us and guide us through life, so we have no need to question their instruction. Titus (1970) stated "Man is not only conscious of himself as an "I," he is also conscious of the fact that it is he who is conscious" (p.150). Searle argued that the "mysteries" of life are caused by biological processes (Searle, 1984).

According to Brill (1995), Freud believed that our dreams were the manifestation of our intellect, and knowledge could be derived from the interpretation of them. Society has been interested in the measurement of intelligence, and therefore scientists and researcher came up with the IQ (Intelligence Quotient) test, a comprehensive test formulated to measure intelligence in young people (Terman & Merrill, 1960). I would like to see the first machine that is given, or that develops a consciousness, I think it would be a great day in science. If the universe is complex and the theory that it was created by intelligent design is true, then I believe the answers to our philosophical problems can be found in a close relationship to nature. This is not to discredit our brilliant scientists, but they have to adhere to results given through experiments and hypothesis proven by the scientific method. There could be certain things in our world which lack a rational explanation by human experiments, thus forcing most scientists to disregard them a mere phenomenon. Scientists take a rationalistic approach. I believe there will be room for both scientist and naturalists, but they will go in different directions. The first axiom of scientific research is "your research is not complete until it is shared with the scientific community." I believe that somewhere, there may be those who have knowledge concerning the origins of the universe, our intended purpose, our relationship with a supreme being, and these "secrets" are to only be shared with those individuals who are ready and capable of absorbing such knowledge. If this knowledge exists, and it would overturn natural laws and expectations from the scientific community, and if it could be considered blasphemous by the religious community, then these concepts are better left to those with a need to know. I believe that science plays an important integral part in our civilization and its progression toward certain truths, but I also see an awakening by those who seek enlightenment by means not derived from scientific principles.

I found an interesting quote from the "father of modern philosophy," Rene Descartes, who stated, "There is nothing which leads [minds] more readily astray from the straight path of virtue than to imagine that the soul of animals is the same nature as our own" (Zeman, 2002, p. 270). Descartes was a rationalist, so he based his philosophy on the epistemological position that only reason will separate illusion from reality; he only believed those facts which could be proven by arithmetic (Soccio, 2007).

According to Adam Zeman, a consultant neurologist and senior lecturer at the University of Edinburgh, consciousness is a direct result from the complexity of the neurological pathways in the human brain. Although Descartes ruled out the possibility that animals could have a consciousness (or soul) similar to humans, recent scientific evidence has been discovered to explain that the consciousness may be created by the brain, which of course animals do possess. They may in fact have a type of consciousness which differs in complexity to that of a human; I would not rule it out without substantial evidence. In the case of certain animals, such as bats, there awareness may be more closely related to the echo they send out which would make their consciousness be spatial, in contrast to our consciousness which is fed by perception and interpretation of our five senses.

Do you think it is the combination of genetic material from our mothers and fathers, or do you think that it could be possible that we acquire our intelligence from an external force? By external force, I mean a collection of all known minds that have lived previously, or even from an unknown higher power.

I've been wondering about this kind of question. Scientists study rats and mice, monkeys and other animals. These animals surely contain a certain type of intelligence. Scientists would agree that they believe man to be an animal. My question is, if they study animals, and man is an animal, wouldn't they be able to tell what the nature of man is? That is, if they even know what the nature of an animal is. I think that animals can think and they have certain instincts that would leave us to believe that they have a consciousness, even on a very minute level, but man shows different aspects of consciousness that leads me to believe that it comes from somewhere other than biological means. I do agree with you that we have the capacity to learn and strengthen our knowledge base, if we are willing to put forth the time and effort.

I would have to say that, although bright and intelligent, younger generations of people, during their inquietude often disregard an older person's wisdom in lieu of contemplating the alternate course of actions to their misguided intentions. It has been my experience that a vast amount of insight can be gained through the teachings of the elderly, ceteris paribus. Older generations have more collective knowledge than we possess, as a general rule, due only to the fact that they have been on this Earth longer than we have; there are exceptions, of course. Younger generations do accept change at a faster pace, until one day they wake up to find that another, yet even brighter, generation is doing the same thing and fighting for the same liberties for which they once yearned. Consequently, we will all be the older generation after we burn off the days of our youth, if we are so lucky. Perhaps we can learn from the older humans, while simultaneously reversing the apathy and disparagement that is being exhibited by those young people who still have life lessons to ascertain. There may be a plethora of benefits to be enjoyed by giving a willing ear to our elderly.

I suppose that artificial intelligence would be outside the boundaries of human nature. According to Searle (1984), research or theories on the mind-body dilemma must deal with consciousness, intentionality (the world apart from the mind), subjectivity (the world from the individual's point of view), and mental causation (our thoughts and feelings and the effect they project on the physical world). In response to your discussion post, there are numerous examples of processes which are outside the realm of human existence, and therefore apart from human biology, *ceteris paribus*.

As a society, we have indeed created technologies that were once material for science fiction writers, but now are coming to fruition. We are at that point were the mechanical entities which we have created will soon have a "mind" of their own, and we will have to deal with new issues, such as, the creation of a machine that can process information critically and think for itself. Have we, in a sense, played God? I do not believe we have; we have used our talents endowed on us by the creator to create complex machines, and thus we have been good stewards of the talents given to us. In contrast, there are those that would use this technology to the detriment of mankind.

We may face other issues, once artificial intelligence becomes conscious. Conscious is defined as being aware, and to be able to think and feel. At which point will those artificially created entities realize that they may be entitled to certain rights, and will we have to rewrite our laws to include them? I wonder if they will scrutinize us as a society for our past and present actions. The mere occasion of thinking about how those devices will react and feel toward us has caused us to think critically about their existence, so even though they are not part of our biology, they are now part of our psyche.

According to Searle, the reason that computers would have a hard time developing a mind as we perceive it is because computers use syntax and our minds use semantics (Searle, 1984, p. 31). I have watched the movie irobot that you mentioned, and I also watched Wally (Not sure on the spelling) where the little garbage collector robot and the roach are the main characters. In that movie, the main point that I understood was that we can rely on computers and automated machines so much as a society that we can become complacent to our overall health and well-being. At this time, I suppose that the only way a computer can feel is by sensors relaying data to the CPU. Take for instance a temperature sending unit on a vehicle. The main computer processing unit can't actually feel the engine warming up, but that sensor sends a signal to a gauge and the gauge interprets the data in terms of temperature (or oil pressure). In a sense, we could perceive that as a "feeling" although different from us actually touching something warm with our hands. Thanks for your reply and discussion.

 As contemporary humans, we do tend to be fixed on our routine schedules and are far removed from the ancient way of thinking, such as the beliefs in the Greek and Roman myths. The myths were propagated during a time when civilization was intimately closer to nature than we are today. Since that time, humans have tried to reason their way out of the "shadows" and become enlightened, arguably to no avail. We have lost a sense of how our world operates and the animalistic connections associated with this new type of "reason."

One of the articles for this week addresses the philosophical implications of us creating and then interacting with computers, or more specifically, artificial intelligence. The article starts out with the premises that the computer is a brain, and that thinking is computing. It allows for discussion whether we can create sophisticated programs which will eventually end up becoming similar to the human brain. "The computer, and its potentials, force us to examine our assumptions about humanity, mind, and language. Metaphors are an integral part of this process" (Gozzi Jr., 1997, para. 24).

I believe there will be a time when artificial intelligence becomes a problem, in that we will have to decide if we should continue looking for logical answers in machines and computers, or if we will return to nature for the answers which may already be available to us.

Scientists would argue that the processes must be testable by the scientific method, religious scholars would argue that those processes must be in accordance with the word of God, or a supreme being, and I argue that the ancient civilizations may have known thousands of years ago about technology unknown to us today that would explain how certain things like the pyramids have been created. Egyptian metaphysics teaches that human life is intertwined with divine life, by means of transformation. According to this philosophy, the physical world is on a different plane than the spiritual world, but each can come into contact through manipulation of the "veil" in the material world (Clark, 2004).

Let me explain how I believe this philosophical belief system can be beneficial in AI innovation and new technology. Perhaps this "veil" can be manipulated by nanotechnology. When dealing with artificial intelligence, keep in mind that all things living contain carbon and all material mass in this world as we know it contains atoms. We all have seen those magnified photos of atoms encircled by electrons moving rapidly, but with intended purpose. What if (and this is only my theory) a scientist, or theologian for that matter, discovered a way to manipulate the atoms in the human brain while simultaneously manipulating the atoms in a microchip (raising the veil of the unknown) and allowed for communication at the atomic level with biological tissue and silicon (similar to the Mind Machine Project at MIT)? Now that is just the beginning. What if that communication was not delivered by standard electrical means, but by an unknown signal generated by the metaphorical "third eye" of the human mind? This would cause an upset in previously perceived methods of communication, and would force society to look inward and accept the possibility that the human mind can in fact connect to the physical world by means of mental concentration. We may be focusing too much on the nuts and bolts of technology to accomplish AI communication and creation of an AI mind, when the answer to this problem may literally be in our heads. One of the biggest obstacles facing AI research and development is lack of funding. The U.S. Navy has been actively involved in AI research with The Navy Center for Applied Research in Artificial Intelligence (NCARAI). Scientists there began researching developmental theories, and most of what has been found out through their research is classified. If any new developments exist, they are most likely applied to our military defense systems (Schultz, n.d.). The United States is not the only country that is interested in AI. At VU University in Amsterdam, their research department consists of an agent systems group, knowledge representation and reasoning group, and a computational intelligence group, which is a new avenue in AI theory (VU University Amsterdam, n.d.). Much of the pioneering ground work has been accomplished by previous researchers. This would allow a new researcher to read and study past theories, and spend more time on new theories and development, which of course, need to be shared with the scientific community if progress is to continue.

Conclusion

In summary, John Searle does not believe in the possibility of artificial intelligence possessing a mind that is comparable to the human mind. The human mind is created through the biological activity of the brain. Andrew Jones believes that it will be possible to mimic or duplicate this activity to produce machine that think autonomously. As more machines and robots become intelligent and move toward consciousness, our conceptions about these devices will change. Many times throughout history, visionaries like Galileo held their positions when trying to convince society that change was possible, and those dogmatic belief systems can be altered. I will try to clarify my response to your question. Knowledge is the state or fact of knowing. It is also familiarity, awareness, or understanding gained through experience or study. Intelligence, on the other hand is the capacity to acquire knowledge and the faculty of thought and reason. Knowledge is something that we can gain or learn, whereas intelligence is a determination of if we are able to receive that knowledge and accept its worth. Titus (1970) stated, "Epistemology, the theory of knowledge, asks 'What are the sources of knowledge' (where does it come from and how do we know this), 'What is the nature of knowledge' (does a real world exist outside of the mind), and 'Is our knowledge valid' (how can we tell truth from error)." This is called the test for truth (p. 24). Knowledge can be gained; we already possess intelligence. Intelligence can also be gained in certain circumstances. Take military intelligence, for instance. Data and information is gained to assist commanders and troops on the battlefield. Prior knowledge is then used to assess, distribute, and react to this newly acquired data to implement into an offensive, defensive, or protective strategy. In terms of artificial intelligence, most of the intelligence hurdles have been crossed, especially with the internet being available for almost immediate download of information of any subject. AI machines may need to be able to tap into this vast source of knowledge in order to properly react to the plethora of intelligence involved in making decisions. To answer this correctly, we must define machine, mind and consciousness. First, a machine is any system, usually of rigid bodies, formed and connected to alter, transmit direct and applied forces in a predetermined manner to accomplish a specific objective, such as the performance of simple work. This came straight out of the American Heritage Dictionary. This means that in the intellectual community and scholarly persons who have agreed to this definition being put into print, the human being sounds much like a machine. Yes, this is an example of twisting semantics around to fit my agenda, but hey, survival of the fittest. The human body is a system. The body has a semi-rigid frame (bones). Our muscles respond to stimuli and demand by increasing (altering) their size to "accomplish a specific objective" we refer to as work. According to my analogy, humans are machines, so premise 1 tells me that machines already have minds.

What is a mind? The dictionary defines a mind as "The human consciousness that originates in the brain and is manifested especially in thought, perception, feeling, will, memory, or imagination. Let me stop here. A human is "of, or relating to, or characteristic of man or mankind; having manifest the form or characteristic of man or mankind." Well, robots have internal cooling systems; so do we. Robots take in data and perform tasks; so do we. If a robot loses its power supply (electricity) they shut down; a human will also shut down if it loses it power supply (food). Robots need lubrication; human joints need lubrication. What makes a robot much different than a human? Humans have a mind. But I just wrote that a mind is manifested in thought, perception, feeling, etc., and machines are capable of those processes.

So that leaves me with the definition of consciousness which is simply the "state or condition of being conscious," which is being self-aware. Humans know that they exist. Robots, to my knowledge do not at this point in time. Robots and machines are not self-aware (conscious or cognizant). If a machine is defined as a robot, coffeemaker, computer, phone, or automobile, then it does not have a mind, because it is not aware of itself. On the other hand, if a machine has GPS capability and enough sensors, it is aware of its location, what temperature it is, how much it weighs, if it is low on "fuel," if it requires maintenance, what company manufactured it; the list is endless. These types of machines fit every criterion that would allow someone to believe the premises which have ended the argument that yes; certain machines have a mind and a consciousness. Food for thought: have you ever used your computer or any other electronic device and it seems like you can't get anything accomplished, then after a brief walk away from the device to think about something else, it seems to work normally? This is why I wonder if our minds are able to somehow affect other objects, and we lack the understanding of how this phenomena works. The modern definition of artificial intelligence (or AI) is "the study and design of intelligent agents" where an intelligent agent is a system that perceives its environment and takes actions which maximizes its chances of success ("Artificial intelligence," 2009, para. 1). With that being said concerning machine intelligence, human intelligence is relatively the same thing. We, in fact, are a body composed of biological "systems" and we perceive our environments, and react accordingly to love, hate, all other emotions and fear and threats in order to instinctively preserve the species. So the difference is in the programming. We are taught from an early age not to touch a hot stove, look both ways before we cross the street, and be leery of strangers. Machines can be loaded up with all of the known knowledge that humans have acquired, but can they sense fear and avoid being injured, kidnapped, or worse? In this respect, humans have an innate ability to process extrasensory data at alarming speed. When in despair, humans have been known to have extraordinary physical strength and cognition. Machines, in contrast, may possess the knowledge by means of large databases, but may not be able to tell when they are being lied to or manipulated, or when they are in imminent danger. This is where, for now, humans have the upper hand when addressing these issues. They have the intelligence to decipher new information, correlate that with old information, and at the same time they have an additional tool like insight, or a "gut feeling." For thousands of years, human beings have been able to think critically, use hand tools, erect buildings and defend their selves against predators. Humans have acquired new skills and adapted those skills into forming useful things such as machinery, innovations, even learning genetic research. I believe that it is important for us as humans to coexist with the animal kingdom. I can see where people may have learned the idea that we have ruling power over the animal kingdom. Genesis 1:26 states, "And God said, Let us make man in our image, after our likeness: and let them have dominion over the fish of the sea, and over the fowl of the air, and over the cattle, and over all the Earth, and over every creeping thing that creepeth upon the Earth." (Holy Bible, King James Version, 1989).

There are many interesting things about all animal species. I do believe that man (and woman) was put on this Earth for a reason, yet I am humble enough to admit that I have no idea what that reason is. I do know that we can learn a great deal from animals. For instance, the apprehension that certain animal species feel toward persons of suspicious demeanor or when animals react to changing weather conditions. I believe there is more to this world than people notice on a daily basis and to say we are able to be at the top of the animal kingdom is just a matter of opinion. Perhaps the animals see us as a hard-to-reach meal with weapons.

I can only theorize that there are numerous occasions on which mental processes have affected our outside world and vice-versa. The belief in a supreme being is something that most human beings take into consideration, yet little tangible proof has been given or discovered. A classical dualist theory would involve supernatural forces that would exist outside of the human biology. Nobel-winning neuroscientist Roger Sperry taught that conscious experiences cannot exist outside of the human brain, but that the brain was in fact capable of causing change within itself through electrochemical activity, thus allowing the individual to experience those things that seem to be out of the realm of human consciousness (Schwartz & Begley, 2002). Some mental capabilities that have been discussed in recent years have been telekinesis, which is moving object by alleged "mind power," with no apparent connection to human biology. These demonstrations have left room for debate as to the authenticity of such practices.

Zeman (2002) stated, "Parasomnias are intermittent abnormalities of behavior or experience during sleep [to include sleepwalking, sleep terrors, or sleep drunkenness]...and can be detrimental to health" (p. 142). Although these symptoms affect our biology, or health to be more specific, we often times dream of future events. These events have not taken place, so how is it that they can be considered part of our current biology?

Carl G. Jung proposed a theory that involves dreams and occurrences in the physical world not attributed to an individual's biology directly but events that occur to that individual and are deemed more than just happenstance. "A statistical, that is, a probable concurrence of events, such as "duplication of cases" found in hospitals, falls within the category of chance" (Campbell & Hull, 1976, p. 505). In this statement, Jung rules out those experiences that happen according to random chance and he was focused on patterns of development that happened in an individual's life that happened more as a symbol of things to come which may or may not be directly related to biology; he called it synchronicity (Campbell & Hull, 1976).

Chapter 14 Metaphor/Humanity

Abstract

Sir Winston Churchill stated, "Continuous effort, not strength or intelligence is the key to unlocking our potential." Science will continue to move forward in search of new technologies and ideas. In recent years, some progress has been made in the attempt to create artificial intelligence. The use of metaphor can be useful in helping us understand the complexities of certain technologies and to define clearly our arguments about moral issues related to super intelligence.

Metaphors provide us with a better understanding of the world by improving our communication. They play an interpretative role in our understanding of artificial intelligence, how we perceive this intelligence, how it can best suit society, and the philosophical implications associated with machines, which possess the same cognitive skills as humans. In persuasive discourse, Gozzi wrote that metaphors provide a platform to help us understand the meaning of higher intelligence created by man, but reaching at least equal status with our own intellectual capabilities. Gozzi realized that once we recognize the computer as a metaphorical brain and that the computer was indeed thinking for itself, it would only make sense to believe that the computer could propagate a mind and function as well as a human (Gozzi

Jr., 1997, para. 3). Using metaphors to compare and contrast the brain and artificial intelligence will help lower the intellectual barriers that one may possess in accepting the fact that there may be a created machine that is as intelligent as or more intelligent than the human brain. A contemporary metaphor is to refer to the brain as a meat machine. In the sense that the brain is made up of living tissue and biologically functions as the center of the central nervous system in the human bodies, one could see how this reference could apply. The outward appearance of the brain is a mere shell of wrinkled meat that has a specific function to human existence. The extraordinary difference between the human brain and a chunk of meat acting as a machine is that for years scientists have studied, operated on and researched this "meat machine." The fact remains that they still are unaware of some of its functions and properties. Additional metaphors that may be useful in understanding the human brain could include computer for the body, CPU (Central Processing Unit) for the soul, wrinkled biological and chemical interface, and BRAIN (Biological Reservoir of Automated and Integrated Neurons).

Discussion

Rodney Brooks stated his opinion that we have the necessary knowledge and expertise to create a robot or other device that could mimic human intelligence, but it will take longer than his lifetime to finish. His work at the MIT lab has been to develop a means of communication in which these machines could relay their "feelings" to humans. Such an achievement can be accomplished in the coming years due to the technological advances in the twentieth century and improvement with microchips and other such processes. As far as machines becoming equal to humans, there seems to be enough evidence to support the hypothesis that one day humans and machines will be on equal playing fields. The question is if these machines will recognize us as their creator, essentially their God, remains unresolved. If this is the case, they may serve us and do our will, or they may rebel against us in an effort to control or destroy all humanity (Spotts, 1999, p. 15).

Victor Frankl would say that being human means being able to love, use talents, and remember all the good and bad times that we have experienced during our lives. Frankl lost most of his family, including his wife in concentration camps, yet he believed he had a purpose to survive and live another day (Frankl, 1959). Searle asks the question about consciousness using the metaphor "grey and white gook," but no doubt believes himself and his readers to be in such a state. He believes it to be a central aspect to human existence (Searle, 1984, p. 15). Intentionality refers to our "beliefs, desires, hopes, fears, etc" (Searle, 1984, p. 16). The subjectivity, according to Searle, is the reality that one individual can believe that a sensation exists, whereas another individual can also experience that type of sensation, although totally separate from the first. In this, we experience life from our own points of view (Searle, 1984, p. 16). According to the concept of mental causation, our thoughts and feelings have a direct effect on the physical world and asks the question of how this effect is possible, given that our thoughts are mental, and our world is physical. The four phenomena make the mind-body discussion difficult, in that most answers to these questions are theoretical. Searle argues that mental and physical processes are both true and consistent, theorizing that artificial intelligence may be possible once we learn what creates the mind from the human machine, the brain (Searle, 1984, p. 27). Searle's conclusions about thinking machines is that brain-based consciousness is different from syntax-based consciousness, but both are possible, given the right programming

(Searle, 1984, p. 39).

Conclusion

After reading the various reference materials on the concept of artificial intelligence, the possibilities seem endless on the subject. If humans can become conscious, and if they have invented the computers that are the beginnings of the processes of artificial intelligence, it only stands to reason that technology will show us a better way to create these machines so they too can experience consciousness. As stated earlier in this essay, numerous ethical and scientific issues may arise such as will those machines view us as their creator, or just another conscious entity.

Technological advances in the automotive industry include electronic databases for ordering parts and advanced robotics to ensure efficiency on the production lines. USA President and CEO of Toyota Motor Manufacturing once stated, "I don't want people to think like a machine." Kitano expressed his concern that with new technology, the human worker can feel isolated and threatened by the possibility of them being replaced by a robot. Kitano feels that new technology, such as robotics, can assist the ageing workforce and cause less physical strain on the human body, while still allowing the companies to be competitive in the global marketplace (Vasilash, 1996).

Mitch Waldrop wrote an article in a 1986 edition of Science Magazine that gives his opinion on the advancement of artificial intelligence. He feels that innovations in AI will be slow and steady in the coming decades, but will astonish scientists as they learn new ways to interact with machines with intelligent attributes. Waldrop believes that innovations in AI will be beneficial to both the human well-being and the economy, but admits that we are years away from the robots we have seen in Hollywood movies (Fredell, 1986).

Another industry where Artificial intelligence is on the rise, but increasingly controversial is the medical care systems. Expert computer systems like APACHE III decide what hospital resources can be utilized for patient care "based on the likelihood that a patient will die." This has sparked controversy both in the AI and the medical community

(Newquist, 1994). Somehow letting a computer decide if a human life is worth saving or letting go seems immoral to me. Artificial intelligence has made prominent advances in the years since John McCarthy coined the term, but humans will need to analyse and forecast the ethical implications of allowing the computers to take over our decision-making processes. We live in an interconnected society, much different than the isolationist society of the early twentieth century. Many people have had to work in back-breaking occupations just to come home to a double-mortgaged home and debt up to their eyeballs; reality in America as we know it. Human beings want to believe that they have some kind of control over their personal lives and the condition that they face each day, in a sense; they want to be autonomous; independent, self-contained and self-governed. People who lack these simple rights or are deprived of such tend to be depressed and are subject to losing their sense of self-worth. Humans want to be more than just a warm body; they want to be counted as a beneficial member of the human race (Nicholls, 2005). The question of what it means to be human has been the conundrum which Theologians have been struggling with for a very long time. The early Europeans believed that to be human meant to build cities and conquer new lands. When they came to America and found out that everyone didn't think the way they did, they were faced with a dilemma. Were these native people less than human in the sense that they merely survived and lived off the land? No, they had their own version of what it meant to exist as human beings (*U.S. Catholic,* 1994).

Does being human mean being able to work, love, hate, learn and use your hands to create things and earn a living? Recent combat veterans have returned to such medical authorities as Dr. Joseph Rosen, a plastic surgeon at Dartmouth Medical School. Dr. Rosen realizes that repairing a torn face, missing eye, or missing limb gives back to the individual something essentially important to them to let them once again feel whole, and in that being able once again to feel accepted in our society and feel useful. Replacing a lost limb with a prosthetic gives an amputee a "frame" on which they can once again help themselves to adjust to their new way of life after such a tragedy. Dr. Rosen has also experimented with "wetware," which is a software interface with living tissue (Brown, 2007).

In conclusion, it appears to me that being human is difficult to define. It is a mixture of thoughts, theories and feelings based on what the individual deems necessary to fulfill their life. Americans regard material possessions and wealth as part of living the dream, while in other countries, being human may consist of having clean drinking water, a little dignity and a place to sleep at night in safety. In my own opinion, being human means being cognizant of how we treat others, taking care of our families, helping our neighbors, being kind to strangers, forgiving those who have caused us hurt, helping the poor and downtrodden in our societies, searching for higher truths, seeking out a better self (a self that would not be ashamed to look at itself from a distance and realize what perception it was giving to those who surround it), and constantly trying to learn from the lessons that life teaches us along the way.

Mind-Body

Albert Einstein said, "The intuitive mind is a sacred gift and the rational mind is a faithful servant. We have created a society that honors the servant and has forgotten the gift." Many questions are still being asked about the mind-body problem. Neural networks, brain function and cognition have led some scientists to believe that the human brain functions much like a computer, in that it can produce output according to the inputted program, yet the brain can learn by ways of neural connections unlike a computer's memory bank. Dualism, a separate mind-body approach to philosophy, has led to the theory that the body occupies space as a biological thing, whereas it affects the perception of the mind, which in turn causes the body to take action (Uzgalis, n.d.). This essay will present different opinions relating to the mind-body question in addition to the student's standpoint on this issue. The mind-body question that has troubled scientists, philosophers, researchers, and others is "The human brain is a complex organ. Is it separate from the mind, can they affect each other's processes, and will there ever be a time when we realize the potential of combining the power of both to become more intelligent and effective as human beings?" David Felten, head of the Department of Neurobiology and Anatomy at Rochester said, "Our grandmothers knew all along that our minds and our bodies were connected, even if the scientific community didn't. We've simply provided irrefutable data showing that it's true" (Thomas, 1997, para 5). There may be some truth to the wise sayings of our relatives who lived in an arguably simpler time when individuals spent more time on thought and introspection about such issues.

The connections and questions concerning the mind and body is not a new science. Followers of the religion of Judaism recognize the unity of the human body and the spirit that it contains or possesses. Judaic healing involves a complete healing, involving both of the aforementioned elements for a total restoration and rejuvenation of the person, as the teachings. This theology expresses the belief that the human organism is one and cannot be artificially separated in terms of spiritual and physical health (Frank, 2009).

The mind-body question has evolved in contemporary philosophy, yet still adheres to the ideas of Descartes. Descartes studied the process of thinking, causing an epistemological turn in philosophy. With scientific advances and the decline of the central authority by the Roman Catholic Church, modern philosophy emphasizes methods, techniques, and more contemporary processes that involve a detachment from historical theories and myths. Soccio (2007) stated that Descartes believed each person possessed the "natural light of reason," and they could approach God on an individual basis (p. 262). According to John Searle's perspective, the brain causes the mind, and mental states are biological phenomena (Searle, 1984, p. 39). He arrived at four conclusions why the human brain and the human mind both deal with the conception of human reality in comparison to a computer program. He stated that computer programs were incapable of causing a mind. Brains, in fact, operate differently from computers. Computers do not possess the amount of causal power achieved by the brain and at this point in our information gathering; we do not perceive there is a machine that has the power equivalent to the brain. He noted in final summation that the brain uses semantics, whereas computer programs use syntax, which are two different ways of arriving at communication and understanding (Searle, 1984, p. 41). Certain scientists believe in the time-honored concepts of terms used in older research. Metaphors can be useful in arguing Searle's point of view. The comparison between the stomach and the digestive process is one example. One must have a stomach to have digestion in biological terms, although digestion can begin to take place in the mouth, and even though we have a stomach that exists, we can still survive without it when mechanical devices are used in medical procedures. The metaphor of the brain being a sort of "meat machine" refers to the biological mass that holds the instrument known a the brain, while being aware that the brain acts much like a machine in terms of mental process and cognition. Scientists who hold traditional views on the mind will have to decide if they will accept abstract theories and new information that will undermine previously held notions of how the brain and mind work together (Searle, 1984, p. 15).

The dualistic view of the brain and the mind expresses the belief that matter (Brain) and abstract (mind) entities are separate, which violates natural and perceived scientific laws (Hanlon, 2009). Andrew Jones believes that the brain and the mind work in conjunction with each other as well as with the soul of the human body. The brain acts as the initial processor of information from outside stimuli, like the five senses. The chemical and electrical activity operating within the internal structure of the brain causes the mind, much like high voltage in transformers causes the "corona effect." Energy ionizes the surrounding air because of high voltage being attracted to ground, causing a breakdown of electrons (United States Department of Energy, n.d.). The human body possesses electrical impulses and acts similar to a capacitor. If Andrew's theory is correct, even in minuscule amounts, at the time of high levels of stress or death of the material body, information remains on the soul as an archaic record. This information will be transferred by he soul to a receiving biological body. Andrew is not dogmatic in his theoretical beliefs and is open to enormous possibilities on the subject. According to the Franklin Institute, the Law of Conservation of matter and Energy states that matter and energy can neither be created, nor destroyed (Chandler, 2002). This strengthens Andrew's theory that the mind is a collection of past minds created by all brains, in that every generation unknowingly passes on the potential intelligence to the next generation by means of energy transfer. This aligns with the possibility and belief of reincarnation of the mind by means of the soul. This idea supports the possibility that the soul's purpose is to transport intelligence and information by means of ether properties to the next generation, or at least to another human being at time of birth, whereas the mind and brain are in the early stages of development. Andrew believes it is possible that the "natural light of reason" that Descartes spoke about is, in fact, the transferred collective energy (Soccio, 2007). The soul can be seen metaphorically as a USB thumb-drive, or a vessel in which intelligence transportation is made possible. The human mind acts as an "organic computer." The mind and body communicate with each other by unknown means, even though the mind is not part of the biological world. A new philosophy has been propagating known as functionalism, which is different in many aspects from the theories of dualism and the standards of materialism. Functionalism deals with abstract thought, in terms of the mind-body question, and it recognizes the potential that such complex "machines" as the human brain can possess. Dualism lacks the explanation of how a mind, which is not physical or tangible, can affect the material, or biological, body. From the functionalists approach, certain concepts will have to be accepted, though not proven, allowing room for much criticism from the scientific community (Fodor, 1981). Andrew believes that this new philosophy will open new doors to previous truths and concepts, allowing a more thorough use of the mind to solve such issues, and less reliability on old methods that need to be revised.

In the next few years, devices will be invented to replace limbs that will be part biological, part mechanical. These will be made available to those individuals who had previously been confined to wheelchairs and unable to walk and be mobile on their own. I believe there will be a breakthrough in nanotechnology that will allow doctors to operate at the microscopic level on the central nervous system, thus making paralysis a thing of the past. These "nanomachines" will also be able to perform surgery to remove tumors. I also envision the possibility of uploading information directly into our brains via computer. These will be significant scientific advances.

In contrast, in the next 50 years, a machine will be completed that will bypass the intelligence of the human brain. It will use the internet for uploading data into its "mind" which will give it the background information necessary to develop a sense of self-awareness. At first, this machine and its creator will be praised for their ingenuity and technological advancement. The machine will be able to answer any question, about anything, learning as it processes the answers to life's mysteries. It will reach a point of super consciousness, where the machine connects to the collective energy in the universe, thus tapping into great reserves of knowledge and inspiration. Artists, innovators, inventors, inspirational speakers, preachers, teachers, and the like will sell everything they own to ask the machine the questions and be provided "Artificial Divine" inspiration. The machine will love the attention. The creator of the machine will begin to worry, much like Dr. Frankenstein, if he or she has created the proverbial monster. A standard will have to be set in order to maintain consistency across technological lines in terms of artificial intelligence and new machines and the law. If we, as a society, are to effectively maneuver through complex legal issues and stay in compliance with our laws and regulations, we may need to explore the possibilities of a new branch of AI Law. This set of guidelines will serve as guiding legal principles for the ethical (is AI entitled to) issues, the legal (What systems of law; common, Napoleonic law, natural law) standpoint, and the moral issues (Biblical, societal, community, and governmental) which will need to be addressed in conjunction with the repercussions of decisions in favor or against AI machines and their creators. We should ask, "Is AI going tom be treated with the same consideration as human beings?" An example of a legal issue would be, "Is an AI machine entitled to compensation if they are arbitrarily injured by another AI machine?"

The social implications of developing machines with artificial intelligence will include a discussion on the role those machines will play in our changing world. As a society, we will have to address the issue of whether or not machine intelligence will pose a threat to continuity. If those machines were capable of essentially stealing ideas, concepts, skills and capabilities from the human race, safeguards would have to be installed to protect us and to ensure our survivability (Epstein, 2000).

Individuals responsible for the information made available on the Hibbard (n.d.) website expressed their concern about the potential chaos that could be created if these machines are created, and we are still in our current legal and economic systems. Their concern was that if these machines take over the job market, there will be complete unemployment in the human workforce, due in part to the machines' capabilities and efficiency, non-existent attrition rate, and a healthy workforce of little concern. We would lose the ability to support our families, and the only people making any significant amount of money would be the facilitators of the machine workforce. According to Hibbard (n.d.), brain capacity may eventually be bought from scientists, which could discriminate against those who have low socioeconomic status, and are not able to download the amount of information required to remain competitive in the job market.

  Another ethical dilemma that we could face would be in the stock market. It is hard enough for the government to keep track of the numerous transactions by way of the Securities and Exchange Commission, and there is still fraud and abuse. These machines could process so much information at lightning speed, and it would be hard to tell if they were conducting insider trading, etc. In contrast, these machines could answer the very questions that have puzzled civilization for thousands of years, such as our purpose here on Earth, and the origin of our species.

Acculturation, as defined in Webster's Dictionary, is the adaptation to a culture, especially a new or different one. It is also defined as a mutual influence of different cultures. In my opinion, if someone is strong as an individual, they can pick up traits or customs of a new culture, but still maintain their unique sense of who they are. For example, I live in Texas, which has a strong Mexican and American culture as well as a Southwest influence. I love Mexican food and I have learned some simple Spanish phrases. A lot of the homes in Texas have Spanish or Mexican influence in their architecture, and they are beautiful. This does not mean that I am going to turn into a Spanish-speaking person, but I enjoy the cultural exchange and welcome the new opportunities to meet different people. At our town hall meetings, various ethnic groups are represented and welcomed. We all have different opinions but the knowledge that we can learn from each other shows that we are keeping or unique culture and sharing some values.

Chapter 15

Critical Thinking and Society

Former Illinois governor, Rod Blagojevich, was found guilty on one count out of a possible 24 in a landmark corruption trial. The American public was awe-struck as the outspoken and genuinely prominent governor left the courtroom. Of course, prosecutors will push hard for a retrial, as they believe Blagojevich should have been guilty on more charges (Harris, 2010). Critical thinking could have prevented this entire episode, as well as good moral judgment. Common sense should let a leading politician know that attempting to sell a senate seat in such a high-profile position would be met with scrutiny and perhaps entail criminal charges to the detriment of the respective political party. It is vital to uphold a political office with the honor that is entrusted to the individual by the American public. Provided the allegations are true, this shows a lack of respect for the constituency, and a lack of forethought in the decision-making process, which would have allowed Mr. Blagojevich to foresee the detrimental impact this occasion would have on the public's view of their elected leaders. Soccio (2007) stated, "[The French philosopher Charles Renouvier (1815-1903) described free will as] "The ability to hold on to one idea among a number of possibilities" (p. 435). Simply put, we have the freedom to choose our own path in life, and it may be possible to "will" ourselves back from an unproductive or depressed state of mind. We must first believe that we have free will [the innate ability to make a choice], and then have the self-determination [drive] to act upon our belief. According to Titus (1970), "Truth is defined as sincerity, honesty, conformity with fact, correctness and accuracy." Titus (1970) stated, "Knowledge is experience that is organized by the self or mind" (p. 39). As we interact with our environments, knowledge is gained. Gained-knowledge is the result of mental expansion, or growth, in which a human being or any "like" living organism with interests and drives interacts consistently with its environment. In the abridged version of John Locke's book, Winkler (1996) stated, "Opinion is admitting or receiving any proposition for true, upon argument or proofs that are found to persuade us to receive it as true, without certain knowledge that it is so" (p. 304). Simply put, it is what we believe to be true due to the processes involved in our five senses.

Developing Awareness

Critical thinking is vital in today's society, due in part to the mass amount of technological information that is present and the electronic communication between businesses. Thinking is not just regurgitating facts that are learned, but a systematic approach to applying those facts with experiences and finding a way to focus when things seem overwhelming. Certain methods of overcoming the hindrances to critical thinking may include, but are not limited to, finding a quiet place to study or ensuring we are taking in a well-balanced diet with regular exercise to maintain stress levels. There are often subliminal undertones to messages that we receive and we must interpret those messages if we are to continue to think clearly. Sales brochures are synonymous with using attractive models to grab our attention, even though they are selling an unrelated product. We as consumers must adjust our preferences and see through the smoke to determine if we really need that product, or if it was a play on our emotions.

We should leave our egos and personal agendas at the door. Most of us have a strong sense of who we are and that may be a hindrance to our accepting new ideas that go against our preconceived notions of the "truth." We should contribute to society and local conversations without being an overbearing and dominating force. This provides room for others to get their points across. We should avoid distractive and unproductive speech, such as "like, you know, man," and other such slang that has no real meaning and only attempts to maintain the audience's attention (Ruggiero, 2009).

Chapter 16 Solve a Problem

We must fact-check our sources prior to accepting the information as reliable. Eyewitness testimonies have been proven to be unreliable due in part to personal biases and emotional interpretation of the given situation. Although subject to the author's opinion and perspective, published sources are a good source of reliable information. Expert opinion is considered to be a trustworthy source (Ruggiero, 2009). Competition can cause several problems regarding truth in media and reporting. Some would argue that competition is good but it can also contribute to cutbacks and lack of funding for media staff, which can ultimately lead to poor quality product (Gentzkow & Shapiro, 2008). Either/or thinking can also cause errors in truths. An example of this is you are either healthy or not. Well, that is left up to the decision of a doctor in most cases, which when evaluating the human body, a large person can still be healthy even though they have a few extra pounds, whereas a skinny person may be skinny due to eating disorders. The person may in fact be both healthy and have a few risk factors (Ruggiero, 2009). Avoiding the issue will not be conducive to error-free thinking. In a trial, if the opposing side has no case, it would not be fitting to attack the opponent just to satisfy the need to defend the respective client. There are many factors that lead to errors but one more is over generalizing. An example of this is all Texans are bad drivers. One may come to this assumption if they were cut off during morning rush hour traffic. One driver acting foolish does not make all drivers in that state terrible drivers (Ruggiero, 2009).

Famous Thinkers - Noam Chomsky Noam Avram Chomsky is a linguist, composer and publisher, and political activist. He was very outspoken about the United States involvement in the Vietnam War or against any nation that he believes tries to force their political or moral compass on another. Chomsky has worked for many years in the field of linguistics, attempting to prove his theories from a biological as well as a psychological standpoint. He theorizes that language will happen no matter how much nurture is involved in the process. Students can learn from a very early age how to construct new words and learn foreign tongues. He argues that language is innate and that it is just another function of the human brain. Regardless of how much is taught to a child, reading to them or otherwise, they will begin to develop patterns of speech and language and eventually begin to master these accomplishments (Source Watch, 2010).

Chomsky's Contributions to Society

Chomsky contributed his theories to society on how a child can grasp the fluency of a language between the ages of 3 and 10. This inadvertently led to his criticism of the modern educational system in the United States, as he expressed dissatisfaction in the fact that language is taught at too late of a point in our children's development. He argues that foreign language should be taught in elementary school, as this is the best time to learn linguistics. The second contributing part of his theory is that a child will begin to develop and use these skills on their own without a trigger or too much coaching from their parents. Certain learning and training aids may be beneficial but are not really required (Crabtree, 1999).

Chomsky's Personal, Social and Political Environments

For Chomsky, students are the best at creating and arguing debatable issues and for those who have an open mind; they are some of the best listeners. Chomsky relished the moments when he could spark critical thinking in the young mind. He told students that most national figureheads are the same as the old one and that they cannot be trusted to operate in a non-tyrannical manner. The facts upon which he based his theory may not be substantial but he was able to begin another critical thinking conversation with American youth. His arguments for Iraq include the fact that the United States government has supported atrocities in the past while small factions of free people were laid to the slaughter. He questioned whether the U.S. could indeed lead a justified war to end the violence in Iraq judging from our past record in political upheaval (Macfarquhar, 2003).

Chomsky's Creative Process

His thinking process was first met with criticism, as with any new theory. He later proposed that a child is ready to master a language from their biological makeup in a process he referred to as L.A.D. (Language Acquisition Device). This aforementioned theoretical plan would explain such things as generative language, or finite grammar, previously mentioned by B.F. Skinner in an earlier experiment. His point was that infants have a predisposition to master a language

(ArticlesBase, 2008). According to an article from the American Academy of Arts and Sciences, Chomsky shed light on the ambiguous field of cognition and mental activity as it relates to linguistics. In his review of B.F. Skinner's work regarding verbal behavior, Chomsky initiated a monumental paradigm shift in the research subject of linguistics and cognitive psychology. His theories earned his research the term mentalism, as compared to behaviorism. Simply put, mentalism involves the belief that we are born with certain innate properties which allow us to master a language or other cognitive process with little or no outside help (Fodor, 2006). Chomsky is a self-described humanist and is noted for his unrelenting attacks on American foreign policy (Source Watch, 2010). Chomsky is credited with inventing modern linguistics as we know it and is Institute Professor Emeritus at MIT (Alternative Radio, 2008).

Kenneth Earl Wilber Jr.

Ken Wilber is an American philosopher born in 1949 in Oklahoma City, Oklahoma. He is best known for his theoretical studies of consciousness and the cosmos, and how these relate to our human interaction and condition. For over twenty years, Wilber has published several books and projects including The Atman Project in 1980 and more recently, A Theory of Everything in 2001. His collection includes over 20 books and research papers. Wilber has integrated such theoretical ideas as previously researched by Sri Aurobindo (Hemsell, 2002).

Wilber's Contributions to Society

Ken Wilber is well-known as an integral philosopher. Supporters claim that he has been instrumental in the field of cognitive and super-consciousness studies in this century. Deepak Chopra suggested that people should read and absorb all that Wilber writes and speaks, as he is very talented and they would benefit from his knowledge (Boulder Integral, Inc., 2010). His theories have contributed to the higher consciousness movement and have been applied to the studies surrounding the behavior of CEO (Chief Executive Officers) of many companies and corporations. The management processes of many CEO's have been studied statistically as well as psychologically and many theories exist about their past and current activities (Young, 2002).

Wilber's Personal, Social and Political Environments

Wilber currently resides in Boulder, Colorado and attends conferences and scheduled meeting where his book sales are in great demand and the questions by many of his fans and supporters are addressed, if not completely answered. He is the president of The Integral Institute. He is quoted as saying to the effect that the spirit sleeps in nature and finally reaches actualization or recognition in differential transparent domains of consciousness (Young, 2002).

Comparison of Chomsky and Wilber's Creative Processes

The differences between Chomsky's and Wilber's theories are as simple as foundational and theoretical. Most of Chomsky's ideas come from the work of other psychologists and big thinkers and from empirical evidence from experiments. In a sense, his work can be quantified or at least tested. Not saying that Wilber is wrong or misguided, but his theories rely on the expansion of the mind and the human ability to accept abstract though patterns as relative truths. Both of these men have contributed a beneficial amount of knowledge and perspective to our society. Critics of both may not be ready for the theoretical knowledge or research that has been the life work of these two critical and famous thinkers. Freud's Drive Theory faded in popularity because researchers were able to determine or theorize that people always had that push and pull on them to succeed or accomplish goals (Reeve, 2009). It's not that we as human beings are sedentary and them due to an external force or stimuli we suddenly decide to move. We are different in that way from a non-human object. The force that drives us as compared to an object is our mind. Our mind constantly evaluates our positions and determines what we need to do next, even when we are asleep. I do not discredit Sigmund Freud like some psychologists do, actually, I have several of his books and I find his writings quite interesting. Most psychologists today would tend to gravitate toward Carl G. Jung; I have a few of his books also. The fact that we are thinking about why we are motivated is a step in the right direction. It is sad to think that someone would be that paralyzed by the fear of the unknown. According to our text, our experiences can be combined and analyzed by four separate parts, including feelings, physiological preparedness, function and expression (Reeve, 2009). The workers feelings were of anxiety and thoughts like, "I need financial security and I need to know exactly what I am getting myself into." The physiological part could be the stress that they were feeling which led to a decision based on how the anticipated move was affecting their well-being. They probably wanted that position so bad, but could not function properly due to the fear of the unknown. They finally had to express to the new company that they could not take the offer. I have known people who could not leave their homes because of fear of what to expect. Most of the time, they could function normally, but there were times when this condition was crippling to them. Our society places certain pressures on us, whether it is to be thin, pretty, handsome, or drive a new vehicle, and this affects certain people more than others.

There seems to be an apparent loss of direction and motivation in certain sectors of America. I don't particularly enjoy paying income tax, but I know that it benefits the common good of this nation. Some people believe that if you don't naturally agree with the total consensus of a particular party's agenda that you aren't a true American; whatever political party you are aligned with. I have a strong opinion on most issues, but I like to hear information from all sides before forming a platform on which I intend to stand. First and foremost, we live in a Republic where a tax law has been passed to provide funding for social security, social programs, and the military defense budget. There are a number of key issues worthy of moot (debate) in this world; a world that seems to be changing at the speed of light. I hope the politicians intend to keep most, if not all, of the campaign promises that were fed to the masses in an attempt to persuade popular opinion. Honesty and integrity are huge motivators, in my opinion. Taxes are probably here to stay. We need to find a way to motivate ourselves to do what is best for our great nation, our communities and our families. In doing this, we can do what is best for the world. I truly pray for America to remain strong, both economically and morally in the coming years so that our children will continue to enjoy the bounty which is so often taken for granted. If we all do our parts, perhaps someday we will all reach self-actualization.

People become complacent in their lives and current activities due to their comfort zone. Change causes an uncomfortable feeling and it scares some people. Deeply ingrained habits become the norm and there is little incentive to address the issues. Different people are at different levels of change. This could be attributed to goals and attempts by the individual to want or need success or achievement. Attitudes, motives and emotions all play an integrate part of change or the resistance to change. If someone desires to change the way they act toward other people, the change may take time but will be reinforced by the fact that the person initiated the change, and they were not forced to do so.

An example where a person was resistant to change is an individual that I previously worked with that had several negative health risk factors. Their diet was poor, they were overweight, and many stressors existed in their life. Their health declined as a result. They expressed to their doctor that they prioritized work and overtime before taking care of their physical well-being. After consultation with their physician and a corporate wellness coach, they rearranged their previous activities and habits, and are now getting in better shape and have quit smoking and started a beneficial, consistent exercise program. Employees work and are productive for reward or because they are afraid that if they don't perform they will be disciplined, or perhaps have their jobs terminated. It is great if employees can come to work because they enjoy what they do, but managers must keep in mind that if the employee doesn't make enough money in today's economy, they will look for work elsewhere. People don't stay at the same job until retirement anymore like in years past (Arzola, 2000).

    Successful employees are passionate about what they do. They have a sense of commitment to the processes that make up a good organization. In an effective organization, every employee feels valued, and individual employees are allowed to take chances when it comes to new improvements and new ideas. This keeps the workplace fresh with inspiration. Employees also like to know what to expect from their managers and supervisors, and the less micromanagement the better (Arzola, 2000).

Employees should seek out their intended purpose in regard to their own opinion. What are they trying to accomplish in their life? Are they trying to accomplish anything at all? Is it any of the employers business? Maybe they are soon to be retired and they feel that they have or have not fulfilled all of their dreams. Lately I have been running into folks with little or no ambition. They are at ease with doing nothing. They seem mighty content in their current walk of life or choice of career, and that's fine, if you're a turtle. They seem to be the embodiment of apathy. College students today have every slice of brand new technology right at their fingertips, and they have the financial means to acquire it. Student loans are given out by the government, and the cycle is apt to continue. What happened to hard times? Are there really any motivators left for this generation and the next? Did they simply vanish into thin air, or were they replaced with something more sinister and vile: the free ride. I would not even consider asking my employer to help me with my educational goals. For one reason, it was my choice to go back to college, and second, it is not their responsibility to provide an education for me. There is a misconception in this country that everyone has a right to an education. Not true, it is a privilege, not a right to advance your knowledge and skills about the natural world, and only by determination and persistence will you reach those goals. I would love to see an uprising in the next generation where younger people begin to believe that personal responsibility and goal-setting, along with hard work will be the only way for them to be effective in our society. I don't need the government or my employer handing me a free ride, but I do appreciate the opportunity to take out a student loan to get to where I am going. As employees grow in effectiveness, a company's leadership team should implement methods of servant leadership to develop skill sets, and by soliciting feedback from employees, the leadership will be aware of potential ideas and improvements to add to the overall environment in the workplace. Some things examples that leaders/managers can do as a servant Leader are interacting with personnel and getting to know employees at least by first name basis. This allows the employee to feel like part of the "company family," not just a number. Managers should be looking for opportunities for success.

Managers have a responsibility to the company, stakeholders and shareholders, and to the employees to maintain efficiency and profitability so everyone who works there will continue to maintain employment. Managers can maintain a balance between individuality and profitability by reward systems and praise when the job is done well. For those employees who contribute less, a coaching program may be implemented to raise their level of awareness as to their responsibilities as employees, and management's expectation for their output. "...Employers use paychecks, bonuses, surveillance, competitions, and threats of termination to motivate their employees" (Reeve, 2009, p. 111). Punishment does not always work as intended. If it is handed out as a means of embarrassment, the employee will become resentful and may cause other employees to hate their jobs. Managers must be aware of the possible repercussions when administering punishment and discipline, as other reinforcements may be used in a more effective way (Reeve, 2009). I like busy work. The position that I used to hold was tough in that we did not produce anything. I supervised several security officers who performed routine daily tasks. They met the requirement by the NRC (Nuclear Regulatory Commission) for physical plant security at a nuclear facility, but it is not like manufacturing where the employee can see the end product of their labor. No products are produced; it is a service industry job. This creates conflict at times with new employees who had become accustom to other types of working environments. I found it to be a challenge to address morale issues when in reality; there was no problem, just boredom. Our management team routinely addressed human performance errors which affected the bottom line of such contract companies and in an attempt to satisfy organizational requirements and benchmarks, past employee briefings did not gone so well. I have sat through leadership meetings where a VP will talk about pride of ownership in our daily tasks, and for the employees, when we tried to relay that message; it was often met with skepticism and doubt. This is where an effective supervisor can speak in the vernacular and let the employees know what management is saying and expects of them, in their language. Employees work for money. If PRP (a type of yearly bonus) is decreased due to an increase in human performance errors, the employees will try harder to meet expectations next year. I also found it a challenge to encourage employees to keep good attendance, because there were other shifts waiting to go home. If there are too many calls-offs, overtime must fill the void, which in turn brings management around trying to fix the issue. Extra money on the paycheck is a great motivator, but there are some employees who will still need extra reinforcement and training to meet expectations.

Workplace Motivation - Social learning theory

Albert Bandura proposed social learning theory. Although researchers credit Bandera with proposing the theory, Chaplin (1985) stated, "Social learning theory grew out of the work of John Dollard and Neal Miller at Yale in the 1940's (p. 433). Cherry (n.d.), "Researchers consider [his theory] the most influential theory of learning and development" (An Overview of Bandura's social learning theory, para. 2). Social learning theory is a collaborative effort from many years of research. According to his theory, people basically learn by watching a behavior. His "Bobo doll" experiments showed how children will carry out violent acts. Adults who demonstrate violence in the home are teaching the same to children. If children see an aggressive behavior, they will repeat it later as an acceptable form of operation. Aggressive behavior shortens shaping timelines. Children can repeat a violent act after only seeing it once. Violence in the home contributes to aggressive behavior on the play ground. Children are always watching adults, so it is vital to keep in mind the attitudes and actions that individuals demonstrate in front of children. In contrast, adults can demonstrate love and affection and make a safe environment for family members to live. This observational learning caused a major shift in previously conceived notions of behavior (Cherry, n.d.). A good example of this type of learning is an elderly person shows the next generation how to do a task. This could be when a grandfather shows his grandson how to plant corn or hoe weeds from a garden.

Performance is affected by a reward or punishment system. An individual can learn to expect certain rewards for actions. If the reward is high enough, people will continue to perform the behavior. This is known as locus of control. In 1954, Julian Rotter founded this observation (Laird & Thompson, 1992).

Performance and Modeling

Benjamin Franklin said, "Experience is a dear teacher, but fools will learn at no other." Franklin meant that there are other ways for a person to learn than just doing it. All five senses should be used when learning to make memories and to solidify the knowledge in the subconscious. Social learning theory involves learning a task or operation and also watching a model that is performing that task. From this, a person will pick up on the correct way to perform a task or craft and he or she can begin practicing to become efficient at that particular activity. This theory focuses on how well an individual learns from firsthand experience and by observation. This theory differs slightly from classical and operant conditioning. According to this theory, it is possible to develop and learn new behaviors without doing the task. I used this type of learning in the military. As a squad-leader, I would study plans and maps with soldiers prior to completing a mission. Soldiers would appropriately complete those tasks because the new information was already processed. Soldiers reduced the amount of time it took to complete the job by learning new tasks ahead of time. This common learning technique is also known as observational or vicarious learning. Participants can learn how to start a car or how to collect mushrooms for food simply by hearing about it or taking a trip into the woods (Morris & Maisto, 1999).

Social learning Theory is a type of behaviorism that explains the relevance of thought processes as provocative operators in an individual's habits. Dollard and Miller theorized that imitation played a major role in the outcome of behavior. Bandura tested and confirmed their hypothesis with a group of experiments on modeling and observation, which used children as learning subjects. These studies showed that children will learn aggression by observing adults who exhibit aggressive behavior. This was an influential finding and proved that an individual can learn a behavior. Behavior is not just a product of environmental influences (Chaplin, 1985).

Modeling

Proponents of social learning theory use behavior modeling to prove that individuals do not necessary inherit violent tendencies. This can be helpful in the field of criminology. Bandura believed that children learn aggressive behavior by observing others, for instance, by watching television, or by their surroundings (Isom, 1998). According to this theory, people learn behavior from the same society that reinforces aggression. Learned helplessness occurs when a person believes he or she has no control over his or her lives. A sense of apathy can set in now. Researchers have not proven this part of the theory by extensively observing childrearing in different households (Laird & Thompson, 1992). Attention, retention, reproduction, and motivation are necessary for effective modeling. Various factors affect attention, including distinctiveness, and prevalence. Researchers measure retention, in that it is vital that the individual remembers to what he or she paid attention. Motivational factors can include rewards and punishment (learning-theories.com, 2008). Researchers can study criminals and individuals who suffer psychological disturbances for deficiencies in social learning. One of the indications of borderline personality disorder is a lack of consistent accomplishments (Freeman, Pretzer, Fleming, & Simon 2004).

Workplace

In my workplace, new hires are brought in to training after a thorough background investigation to ensure trustworthiness and honesty. I have never heard it called social learning theory, but it is obvious that management uses the theory at the plant. Management requires new hires to go through career-based computer training, annual firearms qualifications and various other duties to become an armed security officer at a nuclear facility. They learn by listening to the range instructors and by reading vast amounts of regulations in preparation for their licensing test. Managers will not assign a weapon to a new employee before the employee completes all of these steps. Once on shift, the new hire will train alongside a more established employee for a few weeks to learn the ropes.

During this time, they will be under a behavioral assessment program because they carry a firearm and they are new to the plant. Our management has initiated a behavioral observation program. Supervisors address management programs that allow continual feedback and the employees are usually very receptive to these initiatives. Management provides employees with full support by to be aware of any questions and deal with any problems that may arise. This helps drive better performance and increased focus on company business.

In summary, social learning theory exists because of years of research and observation. People learn by watching other people perform a task. When society exposes children to aggressive behavior, the children will repeat that behavior. Previously, researchers believed that people inherited aggressive behavior. In the workplace, this theory can provide a platform for new employees to learn by observing their mentors while conducting on-the-job training. Employees learn by watching other employees and this allows them to solidify the action and become more effective. Employees can learn how to do a task before they complete it by reading about it or watching a film. In contrast, if an employee believes that he or she is helpless and conditions will never change, there will be a loss of motivation and production output. Older or well-established employees act as models to new employees in an organization. Managers can use modeling in which an employee may be afraid to learn a new task. The employee can learn by watching another employee who will encourage and help the employee to cope with workplace anxiety. This can be helpful in law enforcement and other dangerous jobs in which managers must desensitize new employees prior to becoming effective at their new tasks. A third psychological need, competence, is the need to be effective, the need to exercise one's skills and seek challenges, and it is a source of motivation for mastering those challenges. When one seeks an activity with a higher level of challenge involved and has the level of skill required to meet that challenge, a condition can occur which has been named the "flow experience." Mihaly Csikszentmihalyi began to research this phenomenon in the 1970's. He interviewed hundreds of people to find out what it meant to have fun. In 1990, he published the book, *Flow: The Psychology of Optimal Experience*, where he described the concept of flow as a state of concentration that involves complete absorption in an activity. The activity engaged in is a challenge to the individual who has a skill level to meet the challenge. This is a necessary condition in order to experience flow. Flow exists when a person is immersed in an activity to the exclusion of all else; it is an extremely pleasurable, if not an ecstatic moment. Here are several examples of the flow state: If you play an instrument, you may have experienced moments of flow when you immersed yourself in a piece of music and felt absolutely at one with it; the notes sounded perfectly, and all outside noises were blocked from consciousness. Or, perhaps you have given a talk on a topic that you know well. At some point in the delivery, you became aware of hitting each point exactly as you intended; your timing in the delivery was perfect; you could feel the audience engaged along with you. Perhaps you have gone to the pool to swim laps. As you swam your laps, you became aware of only your own breathing and the rhythmic stroking through the water; you felt tireless and at one with the water. You felt like a master of the pool and of your own limitations. All of these are examples of the flow state. *A motivating work environment can allow opportunities to experience flow.*

I believe that my managers have respect for me as a person, and that they know I will supervise employees in regard to company expectations. After that, there are times when I feel my opinion is grouped into a pile with other opinions, and many times I receive a generic response to my suggestions. I have reduced the numbers of good suggestions as a result. About two years ago, we received a new management team from out of state. The two individuals, one for the client and one for our company, make up what they feel are the "brains" behind the operation. Since they have come into our company as leaders, attrition level has risen dramatically and employee morale has decreased. This decrease in morale is a direct result of a condescending attitude from our managers and employee mistrust of their leadership.

Organizational Psychology

Organizational psychology is a branch of scientific study that allows researchers the opportunity to fully understand the behavioral aspects of individuals involved in organizational situations (Jex & Britt, 2008). The behavior and attitudes of individual workers can directly affect the conditions in the workplace. By scientifically studying these attributes, and determining the cause of adverse or positive conditions, organizations arrive at a clearer picture of the mental health of their employees and the affect it has on productivity. When questions arise regarding the validity of theories and structural models in the workplace, organizational psychologists assist in investigations of current processes and in some cases, design new theories. The old way of doing business does not always work in today's connected global environment.

Organizational psychologists improve productivity by assisting organizations with new processes and methods of operation. These psychologists use many resources during the course of study like established models and statistical data. Industrial/Organizational psychologists focus on model testing, statistical research conducted in the workplace, and statistical analysis of results. Psychologists suggest to the organizational leaders a recommendation for the best course of action, or implementation of a new plan to increase productivity and efficiency (Jex & Britt, 2008).

Role of the Organizational Psychologist

The role of the organizational psychologist has changed exponentially since the 1920s. In the early part of that decade, Elton Mayo and a group of his colleagues conducted an experiment on the advantages of proper lighting in the modern workplace. During the Industrial Revolution, factories, and workplaces were dangerous and consisted of poor working conditions. This included dimly lit factories and dusty manufacturing plants. Psychologists proposed a theory that adequate lighting could affect the mental condition of the American worker. Psychologists conducted the study at the Western Electric Hawthorne plant, therefore giving to the experimental name of the Hawthorn effect. The study proved that an increase or decrease in lighting in the work area would positively affect production output, providing some change took place. Another role of the organizational psychologists is to find and eliminate problems associated with attrition rates, employee well-being, and other factors that affect productivity in organizations (Morris & Maisto, 1999).

Psychologists collect statistical data and analyze it for trends and associations with regard to behavior and organizational productivity output. Psychologists conduct thorough investigations in workplace environments to find root causes for lack of motivation, turnover of employees, and ways for the company to increase profit margins by assessing worker behavior. Investigations of research questions are often used to test existing theories and provide feedback on behavioral observation of employees, including extensive model testing (Jex & Britt, 2008).

Uses for Research

Organizations can use research data and input from psychologists to help in team development and work group functionality. Another way organizational psychology can assist companies is in the standardized self-reporting measures, and the comfort ability of the average worker in regard to these methods (Jex & Britt, 2008). Employee participation in groups and workplace activities is essential to a well-rounded organization and the well-being of the employee. "Psychologically, we have to share in the activities of an organization before we feel that we are a part of it. In the same way, we have to share in the life of a community, or we may feel apart from it" (Foster, 1961, p. 368). Researchers conduct experiments at various locations across the country to include college campuses. In Rodger

Griffeth's Research Lab, students are currently studying attrition rates, using the Turnover Events and Shocks Scale (Tess) (Warren, 2009). Psychologists consult various firms, community organizations, and universities (Society for Industrial and Organizational Psychology, 2009). In summary, organizational psychology is an important branch of scientific study that offers employers options and new methods regarding worker productivity and output. Model testing and statistical analysis are key ingredients to the success of research in this area. Organizational psychologists make recommendation to employers for direct change and course of action in regard to a worker's behavior and expanded productivity levels. Theories like the Hawthorn Effect were the direct result of dedication and attention to detail in research methods by psychologist in the field. Organizations can benefit from the research findings of organizational psychologists, in that the attitudes and behaviors of the individual employee have a direct correlation to the organization's success. Proper mental health and employee satisfaction are two beneficial conditions conducive to high levels of productivity and a positive effect of the bottom line. Three reasons for appraising an employee's performance are to (1) determine their declarative knowledge, to test their level of (2) procedural knowledge and skills, and to ensure they are attempting to reach or have reached a high level of (3) motivation. Declarative knowledge is what the employee knows about their job and their surroundings, in regard to the tasks performed on a daily basis. It also allows the employer to assess the employee's understanding of certain tasks required by their position in the company, and to allow for the possibility of promotion by merit and accomplishment (Jex & Britt, 2008). Most employees will reach that "plateau" where they are proficient at their specific job or duty task. At this point, the employer needs to know where the employee stands on their procedural knowledge and skills as it fits into the company's process design. The employee who has reached this stage knows what needs to occur on their shift, why it needs to be done, the impact of their job duties on the company's survivability in the marketplace, and can give honest and accurate feedback on improvements in the workplace. They have become integrated into the company's potential profit-earning environment (Jex & Britt, 2008).

"Effectiveness is defined as the evaluation of the results of an employee's job performance" (Jex & Britt, 2008, p. 97). After spending a period on the same job, in the same position, under the directive of the same supervisor, management needs to be aware of employees who are highly motivated, and those employees who may need a little coaching or supervisory interaction (Jex & Britt, 2008). I believe all three reasons for performance assessments are vital to a company's success, but I would choose to focus on the employee's level of procedural knowledge and skills. After a time, an employee should learn to be proficient at his or her job. There is usually a training and probationary period; a period of adjustment. After this time, the employee should be expected to handle the responsibility of their specific job requirements. If they are lacking in one or more areas, then a performance evaluation can let their direct supervisor know of the deficiency. Supplemental training can be conducted to fill the knowledge void and bring the employee's performance up to standard. In contrast, performance evaluations are subject to the feelings between the employee and the one doing the evaluation. The employee could be a Saint, give to the poor and save a bus-load of Nuns and puppies on the way to play a benefit concert for the Salvation Army, but if their performance evaluator has a personality conflict with them, they could end up with a low evaluation score. Employers may need their employees to peer-coach and conduct training at that level. A thorough measurement of job performance can help to identify strengths and weaknesses by allowing the employer to recognize which employee would be best suited for a specific task. The text identifies these performance measures as organizational citizenship behaviors (OCBs). "Research into OCB has focused primarily on understanding the factors that lead employees to perform OCBs." (Jex & Britt, 2008, p. 96). The advantage of using objective measures of performance could be the identification of the best salesperson out of two adequately performing individuals. Both employees could be perceived as beneficial to the company in terms of output and production, but clearly defined attributes may set one apart from their co-worker. Another reason for conducting performance evaluations is utility. This is where an employee shows a given level of performance, but their effectiveness could be low in other areas. Employees may be able to control their production output, but they still may have a problem with end-product quality and control measures (Jex & Britt, 2008). To influence commitment of employees, an Organizational Psychologist must understand the reasons for certain behaviors in the workplace. Organizational Citizenship Behaviors (OCB) are typically those not included in an employee's job description, such as pitching in where there is a lack of training, helping another co-worker without being told to do so, and projecting a professional personal image to others. These behaviors occur with or without reward. Researchers theorize that the primary reason employees engage in such positive mannerisms is for the positive affect and increased job satisfaction. Organizational treatment of employees can have an effect on OCB, as well as the individual workers' personality traits (Jex & Britt, 2008). Three forms of productive behavior seem to occur in formal organizations. These are; job performance, Organizational Citizenship Behavior (OCB), and innovation. A few ways that an Organizational Psychologist can influence organizational commitment of employees is by analyzing reward systems, conducting research on the temperament of management and employees and how they feel about the company (do they feel like part of the team, or an outsider), and employee roles in the organizational decision-making process. The well-being and satisfaction of the average employee can be a determinant of how effective their job performance will be, and how often they volunteer extra skill sets and training to their co-workers to make the company run smoothly. Simply asking an employee their opinion or how they feel about a new change may make them feel involved and appreciated (Jex & Britt, 2008).

Productive and Counterproductive Behaviors

The relationship between productive and counterproductive behavior in modern organization can have a direct impact on organizational productivity and survivability in the global marketplace. If an organization does not put control measures in place to avert negative behaviors, or reward positive behavior, an internal breakdown of the workforce could impede productivity. The business environment has changed because of an increase in technology and a demand on employee training departments to ensure workers remain competitive in regard to skills. Many job positions require a higher degree of technical proficiency, and in turn, a need for performance appraisals as a way of assessing individual effectiveness. Productive behavior is "employee behavior that contributes positively to the goals and objectives of the organization" (Jex & Britt, 2008, p. 96). Employee behavior and job performance is different from effectiveness, productivity, and utility. A worker may meet certain standards of the company or organization, but may be lacking in terms of total output or quality of product. Utility can affect the way an employee's effectiveness occurs in the company by the way the company values certain aspects of the job (Jex & Britt, 2008, p. 97). Job performance is the most common form of workplace behavior. Two other forms of behavior are Organizational Citizenship Behavior (OCB), and innovation (Jex & Britt, 2008, p. 128).

In contrast to productive behavior, "Counterproductive behaviors are employee behaviors that intentionally hinder organizational goal accomplishment" (MacLane & Walmsley, 2010, p. 62). According to a PowerPoint presentation from the University of Central Florida (2009), these behaviors can include workplace deviance, misbehavior, and subversion. If an employee knows his or her job is in jeopardy, sabotage may be a risk (MacLane & Walmsley, 2010, p. 62). Counterproductive behavior can affect employee performance, attendance, attrition, and general well-being. In extreme cases, hostile work environments can be a source of negative energy that can lead to complaints. Power must be assessed, and in some cases redistributed when an organization attempts to establish programs in the workplace. These programs can include training, assessment, and organizational goals. In most cases, management provides a false sense of participation in regard to employees developing direct influence over decisions and changes in policy (Levitan & Werneke, 1984, p. 5).

Examples of counterproductive workplace behaviors are property deviance (causing harm to company property), production deviance (an attempt by the employee to slow down efficiency), political deviance (directed at other individuals), and personal aggression (hostile actions both verbal and physical involving coworkers) (University of Central Florida, 2009, slide 16).

The Kerns (2009) website explained how happiness directly affects worker performance. Managers can continually assess the mood of the workplace and try to change certain conditions to keep their employees thinking favorably about the organization. Psychologist will complete a periodic and anonymous survey to arrive at an assessment of each individual's attitude toward the company and its performance level (The Performance – Happiness Matrix, para. 1-2). In certain cases, an employer will terminate an employee for adverse behavior. Employers can be discriminatory in the hiring process to combat potential wrongdoers and bad employees. "An employer may defend against a claim of disparate-impact (unintentional) discrimination by asserting that a practice that has a discriminatory effect is a business necessity" [requiring a High-School diploma] (Clarkson, Miller, Jentz & Cross, 2009, p. 712). This is not to say that just because a person has a High-School diploma that the will be well-adjusted to the workplace. Managers can implement strategies to increase productive behavior in the workplace. Pre-job briefings are a way for supervision to have daily communication with employees and keep them aware of changing work conditions. Suggestions and complaints can be addressed at these meetings. A way to decrease counterproductive behavior in the workplace is by rewarding good behavior, and by trending the bad behavior by means of recordkeeping and counseling. Counterproductive behavior has a source. That source could be family issues, money managements, or general dislike of a particular job. Attempts to control such aberrant behavior will increase a company's effectiveness and worker satisfaction rate. Failure to address these issues will lead to deep wounds in employer/employee relationships and can cause loss of profits for the organization.

In summary, productive, and counterproductive behaviors affect organizations and businesses. Performance evaluations can determine which behaviors are profitable for company success. Workers who continue counterproductive behavior will continue to affect profit and productivity of businesses. Managers can take steps to avoid costly behavior by addressing such behavior early. In order for a company to be competitive, managers or supervisors must conduct periodic assessments of employees.

I would use a Need-based theory to guide my managerial actions. This theory builds on Murray Maslow's hierarchy of needs model, where certain needs must be met in order for the individual to "climb" to the next needed level. Employees will not be happy or efficient if they have problems at home which need to be addressed. Furthermore, if that employee is unable to meet their basic requirements for a comfortable life, they will be distracted with stress and worry, and will not be able to perform their job functions (Jex & Britt, 2008). When I got out of the Army, I found a job as a mechanic. One of the guys I worked for walked to work every day. One day it was raining, and I asked him if he needed a ride home. He told me he didn't have a home; he had been homeless for over two years. I was shocked that the boss was unaware of this man's condition, and didn't seem to care as long as he showed up to work on time. Needless to say, I helped the guy find a cheap house to rent, even though he couldn't afford a phone or much else for about 3 or 4 months. After he got settled, his whole attitude changed at work, and he was able to earn more money from commission, because he got his pride back. If I were a manager, I would ask questions about my employee's lives, because after all, their lives affect their job performance. Transformational Leadership is a style in which a person possesses an enormous amount of charisma, intellect, vision, and presence. This type of individual can "move" people when they speak, they can affect people by their actions, and it would appear that they were a natural born leader of people (Jex & Britt, 2008). Cox (2007), "Transformational

Leadership is about leading with an integrity and authenticity that resonates with others, and inspires them to follow" (How does a Transformational Leader work? para. 3). A terrible example of a transformational leader would be Adolph Hitler. He had a striking presence, was able to motivate people to side with his horrendous points of view, he led millions into committing heinous crimes against the Jews and humanity. A good example of a transformational leader would be Ronald Reagan. He was a natural talent for communication. He used to look straight into the camera and when he gave a speech, you felt it. Of course, he was a professional actor, but aren't most politicians? There have been so many examples of transformational leaders in the past, including Dr. Martin Luther King Jr., and I believe Mother Theresa would have fell into this category. Groupthink is where "strong pressure to perform prevents people in a cohesive group from expressing critical ideas of the emerging consensus" (Morris & Maisto, 1999, p. 606). In this condition, good ideas may not be expressed and the results can sometimes lead to disastrous consequences. Groupthink became part of research language in 1971, but I found an interesting portion of an old textbook that is sort of a precursor to the concept. "The emotional climate must be such that the pupil is free to express opinions that conflict with those of the teacher and of his classmates" (Cronbach, Hilgard, & Spalding, 1963, p. 501). In this book, printed almost a decade before the current definition of groupthink came into the forefront of scientific research, the author explains how a group can form an opinion, essentially squashing the view of the individual for fear of retaliation or embarrassment (Cronbach, Hilgard, & Spalding, 1963). Groups can avoid groupthink by setting limitations and allowing each individual to express his or her viewpoints. After careful consideration of all the facts and ideas, anonymous voting can take place where each member is shielded from repercussion that can occur if others know how they voted. According to Brown University (n.d.), groups can be diverse by means of "a shared language, history, geography, [or] physical characteristics" (What Is Cultural Identity? para. 1). Scientist from different backgrounds and diverse conditions tend to move toward decisions as a group, such as temporarily determining Pluto was not a planet, or by trying to convince the world that global warming has man-made causes.

Organizational Development

The organizational structure of an organization directly and indirectly affects employees and stakeholders. Employees first notice this effect as they are assimilated into the organization during the initial phase of employment. Organizational theory is a way of explaining the process of motivation and factors in the workplace. Organizational charts explain the different levels of management and leadership in an organization. Researchers and organizational psychologists continue to refer to organizations as biological processes or machines. Organizations and their processes are so complex, it takes all parts working together to reach common goals and objectives. Leaders allocate enormous amounts of money in an attempt to understand the inner workings of such organizations (Jex & Britt,

2008).

Teams can affect the efficiency of the organizational process. Problems exist in any organization and managers must deal with these problems accordingly. Contingency theory is the main model that is used in organizational design in the modern workplace. This theory involves team-based organizational structure, matrix organizational structure, and the virtual organization. The culture in an organization involves a model of combined beliefs and assumptions and affects the behavior of all members. Every organization is different, but some serve as an example of effective cultures (Jex & Britt, 2008).

Employees will be more productive in a friendly, encouraging work environment in which management allows feedback and individual opinions. Change in an organization can only take place if leaders and managers allow the smallest voice to be heard, and are humble enough to admit when mistakes have affected process development (Jex & Britt, 2008). According to a PowerPoint presentation from the University of Western Ontario (n.d), classical theories of organizational management include Taylors Scientific Management and Weber's Bureaucratic theories. Weber's theory involves establishing order and increasing fairness and openness in employees. Another aspect of this theory is the division of labor by simple and routine tasks. Bureaucratic theory seeks uniformity and a strict organizational process.

Critics claim that this theory is too rigid. Other theories include McGregor's Theory (X and Y), and Likert's System. McGregor's theory explains how people do not enjoy their jobs, they work for one primary reason; money. In contrast, employees want to believe their basic needs will be met (University of Western Ontario, n.d).

In summary, management should create an environment that respects and nurtures the individual worker. Different theories and models can be applied to find which will be the most effective for the particular organization. Models too rigid can cause animosity and oppression in the workplace. A leader will recognize the best method to implement in his or her organization.

Chapter 17

Individual Strengths and Problem Solving Techniques

Team Members and Leaders

In High School, I was heavily involved in the Future Farmers of America. I began my membership in the ninth grade and continued on until graduation. During this time, I experienced group dynamics, public speaking (prepared and extemporaneous), cattle and crop judging, parliamentary procedure techniques, and a variety of other life-learning skills. At times, there were conflicts that arose from personality differences and competition within the group and with students from other schools. Most conflicts were resolved easily, but a few times the arguments or disputes escalated to a walk around the back of the school to settle the differences.

According to the text for this class, group task roles deal with the end product and how each member can affect the outcome by their different job or personality. Group maintenance roles, on the other hand, deal with the continuity of the group, how it is arranged, and the interpersonal relationships that build group cohesion, cooperation, and ultimate success or failure of the task at hand. The agriculture teacher was definitely the encourager-supporter and the initiator for the group. He set the lesson plans, taught the class, and organized the field trips and on-site performances (judging events) and other duties. The encouragement that we received was in the form of a grade and various awards.

At the end of each year, the teacher organized a banquet dinner where the parents could come and watch their respective child be adorned with the awards and have a nice meal. We had several officers ranging from president, vice-president, reporter, secretary and sentinel. I held the offices of reporter, district reporter, and chapter vice-president. In my four year tour, I also went to the state convention with one of my speeches on the necessity of agriculture in a changing marketplace (Engleberg & Wynn, 2010).

The various offices included a variety of duties. The reporter was no doubt the information seeker. When I held that position, I went to various schools and interviewed the FFA members and staff. I also took pictures at the events and circulated a monthly newsletter that was quite informative. The vice-president presided over meetings when the president was absent (most basketball players had games to attend). The vice-president was the coordinator along with the teacher and could be considered the chairperson when a tie-vote was cast over various topics. During the winter months, we sold fruit and the vice-president was in charge of the money collection and coordinating duties with the trucks from Florida or California to speed the delivery schedule. The sentinel sat near the door and resolved disruptions at the meeting. He or she also opened the door for distinguished guests and passed out any paper documents for all members to review. The sentinel's job was to make sure no one disrupted the meeting. In the eighties, you could still get away with physically removing someone from the room.

I was involved in FFA for a number of reasons. That organization is beneficial to anyone who seeks leadership training at a young age. It definitely prepared me for military service and taught me the importance of working with a group and accomplishing goals. A good leader has vision, creativity and motivation to accomplish the task at hand. He or she also has the know-how to impress upon others the importance of completion in regard to work-related issues and the experience we all learn while doing so. Of course, a good leader must also be a good communicator. If you are in a leadership position and you cannot get your point across to the average employee, the mission will not be accomplished and even though you may be intellectually right for that job, others may view you as incompetent (Larson, 2007).

Dealing with difficult members of a group causes other challenges to arise. Group members can chose to ignore or accept someone's bad or disruptive behavior, but that really does not address the issue. Depending on the speaker and the situation, the disruptive member can be confronted either by singling out that member or by taking them aside and counseling them in a non threatening way. The member can also be excluded from the group altogether. If this happens, other member may be forced to have a higher work load (Engleberg & Wynn, 2010).

In summary, many organizations like the FFA can teach young people leadership skills that will help them out later in life. Groups can present challenges to members and observers.

Secondary Data

Depending on the research project or course of study, it may be easier and more conformable to use an encyclopedia as a secondary source. The main reason is that someone else has taken the time to assimilate and break down the massive technical jargon often found in primary research data and it is easier to compile a new perspective from that view. Managers could use the human resource analysis of the employee assessment in determining if more training is needed or if there is a problem with employees getting along with each other. Certain regulations such as HIPAA laws may restrict the manager to not being able to view primary data that is collected from employees; only secondary summaries (Cooper & Schindler, 2006).

Problems Associated With Secondary Data

Newspaper articles would be considered as a secondary source. In instances like this, the data that the reader receives may be correct, but it may not contain the "whole" story. The story may be affected by the individual journalists or editors' political or emotional bias toward a particular topic. Another example could be an advertisement for a company in a flyer. It may claim that the company is "number one" only in reality; they may be number one in the eyes of a few customers who have submitted testimonials to that fact. A researcher can overcome these obstacles by collecting facts and several secondary sources that are not closely related to the secondary source, and by cross-referencing this data with at least a few primary sources (Cooper & Schindler, 2006).

Qualitative versus Quantitative Research

Qualitative research can involve a plethora of data collection techniques, all of which can be useful in arriving at an intelligible solution to the research process. Focus groups are used in managerial meetings to brainstorm and to sort out problems. Behavioral observation can be used in the workplace to determine metrics and efficiency in work output. It can also be an indicator of worker fatigue and safety related concerns. In contrast, quantitative research involves a newer, modern approach to data collection. This is a precise method of measuring consumer attitude toward a product or behavior and what causes employees to react to managerial change. This type of research is typically used to test a theory that has been put into place for a while. In this type, the involvement of the researcher is limited so as not to adversely affect the data or skew the results. Consistency is very important in quantitative research, whereas in qualitative research the same does not apply (Cooper & Schindler, 2006).

Qualitative Research Data versus Quantitative Research Data

Qualitative research data is used to interpret a situation. Such as, the employee hit the other employee because he was either tired or frustrated, or it was in self-defense. Quantitative data would describe the incident in detail, explain to the human resources department the details so they can adequately deliver a synopsis of the punishment and disciplinary action, and it could predict if the incident would indeed occur again at a later date if both employees were allowed to remain working for the company. The data analysis of qualitative research is ongoing and dynamic, whereas the qualitative research design model calls for order and exactness (Cooper & Schindler, 2006).

Scenario

I would try to understand the demographics of my marketplace. There may be an analysis of electrical plug-in outlets, consumer confidence in the new product, and parts availability for the repair and replacement involved with customer service. I would suggest a pictorial model to be created of the business plan so all employees could share in the vision. There must also be a constant feedback loop for new suggestions in the planning process. I would suggest to keep the sample size relatively small so new ideas could precipitate throughout the organization.

One "take away" is the importance of qualitative research and the analysis involved in the process. Qualitative research by definition brings order to all of the data that is collected, although the research involved has little structure and it is very time-consuming. It is not necessarily linear in any approach; it is similar to free association in that it can aid in the collection of many steamily unrelated facts and end with a whole picture of the research project. I just spoke with a veterinarian friend of our family last night and she was talking about how she wished she had paid attention to the research part of vet school, because once she started her practice, she found a new respect for those who take the time to do research that makes her job easier. It was cool to be able to talk about what I learned in this class with a true practicing professional who values good research! Metaphorically, the textbook author compares qualitative research to the moment of fishing, not the details involved. Another good comparison is the mood of a town or city, notwithstanding the many facets that make up the particular city. Another good "take away" is the importance of primary and secondary research and how this can be applied to newcomers or new employees in a company. This research can be conducted by the company's human resource department (HR), or by a disinterested third party. I have always thought that was a funny name, "disinterested," because I would want an "interested" person conducting research at my company. The reason to use a third party is for a non-biased result and so they would not be influenced by anyone at the company. This research can be vital to promotions and terminations if the research finds discrepancies that have led to low morale and employment problems. I can see the usefulness of observing employees in a job where the public safety may be in jeopardy if the job is not conducted according to regulations and procedures. The difference is, at that nuclear power plant, every employee and contractor was made aware of the behavioral observation program and aberrant behavior mitigation program prior to coming on the job site. Where I do have a problem is when I hear about employers who abuse this privilege of observing employees for their own personal gain or enjoyment.

Mahatma Gandhi once said, "No culture can live if it attempts to be exclusive." Gandhi knew that for our own culture to survive, we would have to assimilate new ones into our society. Prior to the nineteen-eighties, The United States practiced a form of isolationism by considering outside entities as a threat, with little interest given to globalization. This isolationism of the past has been replaced by a multicultural society which seeks to bring together all cultures and enable us to experience the contributions of such a mix. In this paper, I will present my own sources of influence, Multiculturalism, and explain how each of these has contributed to the way I view the world and conduct my daily life.

Sources of Influence

The most important people in my life who have shaped my personality and contributed to my knowledge of the world around me are my grandfathers. The formidable years in a person's life make all of the difference in how they will respond to sociological stimuli in their future. My grandfathers taught me to respect my fellow man and the land in which we live. Other ways a person can be influenced in their culture is by the church they attend, the school where a person receives their education, and friends and relatives that they encounter from an early age and throughout their lifetime. One source of influence is culture, which is learned. As a child, I learned my behavior from other people, and I also learned from experience. I learned from my mother and grandparents what was right and wrong.

My paternal grandfather was a Mason, so he was constantly teaching me things and showing me symbols that most people take for granted. To this day, I can still see certain symbols in architecture and paintings on walls when I walk around a city. During my enculturation, I learned a set of core values such as my Puritan work ethic, how to be an individual and still contribute to the community, how to set goals and achieve them, and how to be self-reliant and live off of the land. My maternal grandfather taught me farming skills, how to fix machinery, how to pick the right mushrooms in the woods and how to identify trees and plants. These elders helped shape who I am today (Kottak & Kozaitis, 2003).

Our culture is rooted in the Midwest, and my Mothers' family has lived in the same area for several generations, since the Swiss settled that area. It is a tight-knit farming community, although the small farms have suffered financially since the seventies. I learned life skills in that area of the country, and from the people who still live there. Symbols have always been a part of my life. I remember from an early age my grandfather showing me things in the farmer's almanac and various Masonic drawings and such. There was an owl on the side of his barn, and I asked him what it was. He told me that the owl was a symbol of wisdom and that I should never stop asking questions about the world around me, because by asking questions, I would be walking down the path to wisdom. He always told me to read everything I could get my hands on, and continue to do well in my daily work. Society is seen not as various traditions blending into one heritage, but as the coexistence of many heritages and newly invented traditions within a single nation-state." This is the best way to describe the place where I grew up. A combination of settler-farmers and old traditions combined and new advances were readily accepted to incorporate these ideas into the community. Our farming culture realized that they could not be exclusive. Even taking crops and produce to market involved interaction with other communities and gathering resources on a national level. Gandhi was close to cracking the glass that separates us as humans with his deep thinking and global perspective. The United States can no longer have that sense of isolationism that separates us as a nation; we must be prepared to compete in the global market place and learn from our minority groups and the innovations that they provide. My sources of influence were primarily family members, but as I went out into the world, I realized how important it is for us to learn from our fellow humans and address our differences. By doing this, we can make our society strong and viable, and learn new traditions, and how to accept new cultures. Managers and leaders should be able to identify diverse situations and act accordingly. Historically, women have made less money for performing the same jobs as their male counterparts. In 1963, the Equal Pay Act was signed into law by President John F. Kennedy to protect the financial interests of women and those with disabilities and to prohibit discrimination based on sex. This law is an amended part of the Fair Labor Standards Act of 1938, both of which are enforced by THE U.S. EQUAL EMPLOYMENT OPPORTUNITY COMMISSION (U.S. Equal Employment Opportunity Commission, 2009). Gender is listed as an internal dimension which can be a factor that affects employee well-being, production output, and confidence in the workplace.

Chapter 18 Value of Technology

Every new advance in technology has the potential to allow spin-off businesses to flourish as a result. Take for instance the gasoline engine. This eventually led to more reliable transportation and regulatory authorities to maintain the highways for automobiles. Other spin-off businesses are motels, automotive shops and gas stations. Technological advances have an impact on the way business models are created. Customer service initiatives have driven business owners to seek out new and innovative ways to deal with consumer complaints and other related issues. One such company has designed a comprehensive solution to technology-based process resolution. NetCracker Technology has been instrumental in root-cause analysis and trouble synthesis by introducing the Customer Impact Analysis Module (CIA). The goal of this technology is to reduce service outages, provide higher-level evaluating techniques, evaluate existing data and reduce cost from consumer complaints (NetCracker Technology Corp, 2005). Information technology is used to store data, manipulate the processing of that data, and in most cases it is used to gather or initiate new information to assist the flow of ideas. The impact that technology has on society has a direct relationship to the need and application of the technology. When computers were first invented, a very large processor was needed which could take up an entire room of a building just to simplify a few short equations. With the invention of the microchip processor, size became smaller and the computation ability increased massively.

Computers are not the only technology that has had an impact on society. Improvement in the plow by the John Deere Company led to faster field preparation. Tractors took the place of the horse-drawn farm machinery. Other such devices that had little or no electrical, albeit no computerized components, have successfully taken their place in the body of technological advances in the last century. Technology can impact a society directly or indirectly. In the industrialized world, crude machinery was turned into manufacturing plants and previously obsolete processes were turned into money-making opportunities (Meadowcroft, n.d.). Technology will impact the customer's decision making ability. Disruptive technology makes the customer think about why they are buying a product, what use it will be to them, and how long it will be of use in the future before an upgrade is needed. Products such as RFID (radio frequency identification devices) tags that are being used by large corporations like Wal-Mart and Target answer those previous questions for the company leaders. The main problem with these devices if the potential impact they may have on the customer's trust as RFID can be seen as an attempt by a company to be intrusive to the common customer. The implementation of these devices changed the business model for the warehouse section of major distribution chains. Even products as small as a can of coke can be tracked by the barcode and the box that contains a larger portion of a product are now fitted with a RFID tag. This will automatically reorder the case of soda once that case leaves the warehouse and is loaded on a truck. This helps inventory management personnel. The impact for the consumer is a more cost effective way to ship and receive products which should ultimately keep the costs down at the cash register (, 2009). Companies have different ways of introducing new products and services to the customer. If the technology is highly secret, like something that will be presented to the military, it will have different protocol that a new product on the grocery store shelf. Electronic business is sometimes considered the least secure method of delivering a product like new software. Encryption software has made this task more secure by allowing the sender to send the software jumbled in code until it is received on the other end. Companies like SecureZip deal with this method of business communication and software delivery. By compressing the software prior to encryption, the company can save on bandwidth requirements. To date, this company has delivered over 150 million downloads to customers and will continues to deliver protected password in a digital certificate. The impact to customers who use this product is the safety of knowing that their data stands a very good chance of being delivered without being subject to hackers and those who steal software for private use (Klein, 2004). Business owners want to be on the cutting-edge of new technology. They must first analyze the cost-effectiveness of new products as it applies to their respective business. Newport Corporation located in Irvive, California introduced new products to their customers in 2004 with hopes of expanding their already exclusive product portfolio. Some of the products they introduced included semiconductor equipment like Performix automated teach modules and an advanced packaging die bonder for microchip placement in a sterile environment. These and other products have been instrumental in the development of smaller components and have made small devices possible in the IT world. To introduce these products, the company had to focus on IT businesses within the industry, as a marketing campaign to and end-user would have been a less desirable use for the money. This example shows how companies can target other companies and save on advertising dollars when the average consumer has no need to know about such complex devices and technology at this level (Motioncontrol.com - A Motion Control Marketing, Inc., 2010).

Some of the determining factors of new product delivery is in contrast to the company's size and customer base. New technology is that which is currently not in use or on display at the point of sell. Managing this new product line involves several scenarios and mass coordination. If a new product comes out before adequate advertising is in place, it may sit on the shelf longer than expected which can in turn give it the reputation of lowered demand. On the other hand, if too much advertising money is used for a product that has a lesser need, the company will lose out on profits and will have to recoup that money by raising the price tag. Products that have been speculated but not released can help the tension grow, which sparks a demand in the consumer's mind. Most product failures are the direct result of improper planning and advertising. If these two issues can be addressed and resolved, a new product has a good chance of becoming a viable end-user product that will last as long as the technology is needed (Advameg, Inc., 2010).

Companies will have several methods for proving the added value of new technology. Statistical data can be very informative if kept on the correct product and demographic. In the security industry, loss-prevention can be measured and can be adjusted accordingly. A high-crime area may need additional security officers and new technology in cameras and security-detection equipment. The value of this method can be proven in real-time by the reduction of stolen goods and property. If a reduction in theft can be proven to the client, the need for enhanced security technology will be an easy future sell (Dickinson, 2007).

There are many ways to add extra value during a business transaction. The impact that this may have on the consumer can drive future sales. Word of mouth advertising is very powerful in today's market, so businesses must be aware of consumer needs and deal with complaints in a timely manner. To some, value may be defined differently than those of a tech savvy pallet. Aesthetic quality may be more important to some consumers than the technological advancements that others are interested in. Some consumers may want to try out a product before purchase. Traditionally, tech companies have not agreed to this method of consumer purchasing because of the risk of breakage or theft. Models can be set up in participating stores and a tech savvy salesperson can instruct consumers on the proper use and benefits of a new product. That way, only one such device is subjected to consumer abuse. A good follow-up is recommended after the sale of a new product. Newsletters can be used, though most new and young people will be satisfied with a text message. If clients are willing, let them blog about their experience and pass along their knowledge to future customers. This can provide testimonials for a new product. Companies can use their websites and advertising to drive sales and stay connected with their consumer base. As always, a refund and exchange program should be put into place that is very customer-friendly. Businesses must outline a good support plan for customers who have specific questions, such as operational problems.

References

About Employee Morale. (2008). Answerbag. Retrieved from: About Employee Morale | Answerbag http://www.answerbag.com/article/About+Employee+Morale/a26fcd00-fe60-3939-fa43-d5121531bf18/effective-team#ixzz0ubWgheXm

Advameg, Inc. . (2010). New product development. Retrieved from http://www.referenceforbusiness.com/management/Mar-No/New-Product-Development.html

Albrecht, S., Stice, ., & Stice, . (2008). Accounting: concepts and applications. Retrieved from https://ecampus.phoenix.edu/content/eBookLibrary2/content/DownloadFulfillment.aspx?url=http://ppdfapp.phoenix.edu/PpdfHandler/.fulfill?assetdataid=953c8e85-0dbc-4885-948c-678026233a43&assetmetaid=f231e944-0831-46a7-8a0e-d329db150d2e&p=1.

Alouise, Nacy J. (1998). RACE, RACISM AND THE LAW . The University of Dayton School of Law. Retrieved from http://academic.udayton.edu/race/04needs/s98alouis.htm

Altinöz, M. (2008). An overall approach to the communication of organizations in conventional and virtual offices. Proceedings of World Academy of Science: Engineering & Technology, 31(475), 7.
Retrieved from http://search.ebscohost.com.ezproxy.apollolibrary.com/login.aspx?direct=true&db=a9h&AN=34101871&site=ehost-live

Arellano, Nestor E. (2008). Eight strategies to build a strong tech support team. ITworldcanada.com. Retrieved from: www.itbusiness.ca/it/client/en/home/News.asp?id=47948

Association for Automatic Identification and Mobility. (n.d.). What is RFID? . Retrieved from http://www.aimglobal.org/technologies/rfid/what_is_rfid.asp

Atkins, P. S. (2002a, December 9). Speech by SEC Commissioner: Remarks before the Investment Company Institute 2002 Securities Law Development Conference. Retrieved February 1, 2003 from www.sec.gov/news/speech/spch120902psa.htm

American Bar Association (2009). Retrieved August 28, 2009, from (1) http://www.abanet.org. (2) http://www.abanet.org/publiced/courts/court_role.html

Artificial intelligence. (2009). Science Daily, (1), 1. Campbell, J., & Hull, R.F.C. (1976). The portable young. New York, NY: Penguin Group.

"Artificial Intelligence." Encyclopedia. Issues & Controversies. Facts On File News Services, n.d. Web. 16 Jan. 2010. <http://www.2facts.com/article/xar151400a>.

Acland, Holly. "Morale boosters." Marketing (1998): 36+. General OneFile. Web. 14 Apr. 2010. Retrieved from http://find.galegroup.com.ezproxy.apollolibrary.com/gtx/infomark.do?&contentSet=IAC-Documents&type=retrieve&tabID=T007&prodId=ITOF&docId=A21204274&source=gale&srcprod=ITOF&userGroupName=uphoenix&version=1.0 Gale Document Number:A21204274

American Judicature Society. (2009). *AJS*. Retrieved September 4, 2009, from http://www.ajs.org/ajs/pdfs/AJS%20Strategic%20Plan%20-%20web%20version.pdf and http://www.ajs.org/ajs/ajs_benefactor.asp

AdWatch. (2010). Conscience-based opt out of post-rape contraception . Retrieved from http://www.ontheissues.org/Social/Scott_Brown_Abortion.htm

Bateman, Thomas S., & Snell, Scott A. (2009). *Management: Leading and Collaborating In the Competitive World* (8th ed.). New York: McGraw-Hill/Irwin.

Bateman, T.S., & Snell, S.A. (2007). *Management: Leading and Collaborating in the Competitive World* (8th ed.). New York: McGraw-Hill/Irwin.

Bateman, T.S., & Snell, S.A. (2007). *Management: Leading and Collaborating in the Competitive World* (8th ed.). New York: McGraw-Hill/Irwin.

Bureau of Labor Statistics. (2003). *Women at Work: A Visual Essay*. Retrieved from http://www.bls.gov/opub/mlr/2003/10/ressum3.pdf

Business Communications Group, LLC.. (2010). SEO - Search Marketing Services. Retrieved from http://www.b2bcommunications.com/services/internet-marketing/seo-organic-search/

Buzzle.com. (2000). Responsibilities of a citizen. Retrieved from http://www.buzzle.com/articles/responsibilities-of-a-citizen.html

Brown University. (n.d.). *The diversity kit*. Retrieved from http://www.alliance.brown.edu/tdl/diversitykitpdfs/dk_cul4-30.pdf

Carnevale, A. P., & Stone, S. (1994, October). Diversity beyond the golden rule. *Training & Development,* 48(10), 22.

Chaplin, J. P. (1985). DICTIONARY OF PSYCHOLOGY (2nd ed.). New York, NY: Bantam Doubleday Dell Publishing Group, Inc..

Clark, R. (2004). *The sacred tradition in ancient egypt.* St. Paul, MN: Llewellyn Publications.

Cornell University Law School. (n.d.). *First Amendment.* Retrieved from http://topics.law.cornell.edu/wex/First_amendment

Cracker Barrel Old Country Store. (n.d.). *Social Responsibility.* Retrieved from http://www.crackerbarrel.com/about-outreach.cfm?doc_id=740

Ethisphere Magazine. (2010). 2008 world's most ethical companies. Retrieved from http://ethisphere.com/wme2008/

Ewing, S. (n.d.). Private Business, Sarbanes-Oxley and . LifeCycle Software . Retrieved from http://www.nawbophila.org/images/private_companies_sox_and_technology.pdf

Gil, J. R. B. (n.d.). Technology and translation (a pedagogical overview). Retrieved from http://isg.urv.es/biau/articles/technology_web_2005.pdf

Kensicki, P. (2010). New ethical guidelines set for insurance pros. American Institute for CPCU . Retrieved from http://www.property-casualty.com/Issues/2010/May-31-2010/Pages/New-Ethical-Guidelines-Set-For-Insurance-Pros.aspx

Ethisphere Magazine. (2010). 2008 world's most ethical companies. Retrieved from http://ethisphere.com/wme2008/

Ewing, S. (n.d.). Private Business, Sarbanes-Oxley and . LifeCycle Software . Retrieved from http://www.nawbophila.org/images/private_companies_sox_and_technology.pdf

Gil, J. R. B. (n.d.). Technology and translation (a pedagogical overview). Retrieved from http://isg.urv.es/biau/articles/technology_web_2005.pdf

Kensicki, P. (2010). New ethical guidelines set for insurance pros. American Institute for CPCU . Retrieved from http://www.property-casualty.com/Issues/2010/May-31-2010/Pages/New-Ethical-Guidelines-Set-For-Insurance-Pros.aspx

Regan, E., & O'Connor, B. (2002). End-user information systems: implementing individual and work group technologies, 2e. Retrieved from https://ecampus.phoenix.edu/content/eBookLibrary2/content/TOC.aspx?assetdataid=0c85207c-4579-445d-b2e5-278c996a3835&assetmetaid=9f9341ec-776c-4a2c-8e8c-422fc4e5f1fe.Reference for Business. (2010). Corporate social responsibility. Retrieved from http://www.referenceforbusiness.com/management/Comp-De/Corporate-Social-Responsibility.html

Roebuck, D. B., & McKenney, M. A. (2006). Improving business communication skills. Retrieved from https://ecampus.phoenix.edu/content/eBookLibrary2/content/TOC.aspx?assetMetaId=6d49af4d-00ca-4123-8e1c-fa2677e35382&assetDataId=73043741-3c6a-4fb5-9699-2a4f842ac506.

Turban, E., King, D., McKay, J., Marshall, P., Lee, J., Viehland, D., (2008). Electronic commerce 2008: a managerial perspective. Retrieved from https://ecampus.phoenix.edu/content/eBookLibrary2/content/TOC.aspx?assetdataid=e497f0b5-a9f3-46b7-aeed-558d28f921d3&assetmetaid=0e9ce580-d3e7-4c97-9958-4b2654e2e98a.

DMSRetail Inc.. (2010). E-tailing and multi-channel retailing. Retrieved from http://www.dmsretail.com/etailing.htm

Pickle, Hal B., & Abrahamson, Royce L. (1983). Introduction to business (5th ed.). Glenview, IL: Scott, Foresman and Company.

Prasad, Ch. J. S., & Aryasri, A. R. (2009). Determinants of shopper behavior in e-tailing: an empirical analysis. Paradigm (Institute of Management Technology), 13(1), 73-83. Retrieved from http://search.ebscohost.com.ezproxy.apollolibrary.com/login.aspx?direct=true&db=bth&AN=39755682&site=ehost-live

Roebuck, D. B., & McKenney, M. A. (2006). Improving business communication skills. Retrieved from https://ecampus.phoenix.edu/content/eBookLibrary2/content/TOC.aspx?assetMetaId=6d49af4d-00ca-4123-8e1c-fa2677e35382&assetDataId=73043741-3c6a-4fb5-9699-2a4f842ac506.

Raffoni, M. (2009). Leaders: frame your messages for maximum impact. Harvard Management Update, 14(1), p3-4, 2p. Retrieved from http://search.ebscohost.com.ezproxy.apollolibrary.com/login.aspx?direct=true&db=f5h&AN=36028781&site=ehost-live

Christensen, J. (2010). Facebook as a Workplace Tool?. Businessweek.com. Retrieved from http://bx.businessweek.com/business-communications/view?url=http%3A%2F%2Fjasonchristensen.wordpress.com%2F2010%2F02%2F25%2Ffacebook-as-a-workplace-tool%2F

Center for Telehealth & E-Health Law. (2009). Food & Drug Administration Regulations Main Page. Retrieved from http://www.telehealthlawcenter.org/?c=120

Med-e-Tel. (2002). Telemedicine. Retrieved from http://www.telemedicine.lu/eng/chap14/c1402_09.htm

State of California: CA.Gov. (2010). Medical Board of California. Retrieved from http://www.medbd.ca.gov/licensee/telemedicine.html

Cornell University Law School. (n.d.). *Legal information institute.* Retrieved from http://topics.law.cornell.edu/wex/Copyright

U.S. Department of Health & Human Services. (2009). Alcatel-Lucent. Retrieved from http://www.accessdata.fda.gov/cdrh_docs/pdf9/K092635.pdf

NCSA. (n.d.). National cyber security alliance. Retrieved from http://www.staysafeonline.org/content/protect-your-business

Turban, E., King, D., McKay, J., Marshall, P., Lee, J., Viehland, D., (2008). Electronic commerce 2008: a managerial perspective. Retrieved from https://ecampus.phoenix.edu/content/eBookLibrary2/content/TOC.aspx?assetdataid=e497f0b5-a9f3-46b7-aeed-558d28f921d3&assetmetaid=0e9ce580-d3e7-4c97-9958-4b2654e2e98a.

Romal, J. B. (2009). Improving professional ethics. The New York State Society of CPAs. Retrieved from http://www.nysscpa.org/cpajournal/2004/604/essentials/p58.htm

Tyson-Chan, D. (2008). Market costs can increase through bad ethics. Investor Daily. Retrieved from http://www.investordaily.com.au/cps/rde/xchg/id/style/4184.htm?rdeCOQ=SID-0A3D9632-358C2ACC

Zarka, H. (2007). Ethical and unethical business practices. Associated Content, Inc. . Retrieved from http://www.associatedcontent.com/article/256353/ethical_and_unethical_business_practices.html?cat=3

U.S. Securities and Exchange Commission. (2002). *Public law 107–204*. Retrieved from http://www.sec.gov/about/laws/soa2002.pdf

Campbell, Joseph (1971). THE PORTABLE JUNG. New York: Penguin Books USA Inc..

Carlson, Richard (1997). YOU CAN BE HAPPY NO MATTER WHAT: FIVE PRINCIPLES FOR KEEPING LIFE IN PERSPECTIVE. Novato, California: New World Library.

Gentry, W. Doyle (1999). ANGER-FREE: TEN BASIC STEPS TO MANAGING YOUR ANGER. New York: William Morrow and Company, Inc..

Lazarus, Richard S. (1999). STRESS AND EMOTION: A NEW SYNTHESIS. New York: Springer Publishing Company Inc..

Carter, Carol, Bishop, Joyce, Kravits, Sarah L., (2007). KEYS TO COLLEGE STUDYING: BECOMING AN ACTIVE THINKER (2nd ed.). , Pearson Prentice Hall.

Gardner, Howard, (1993). FRAMES OF MIND: THE THEORY OF MULTIPLE INTELLIGENCES. New York: Harper Collins.

Gardner, Howard. (1993). MULTIPLE INTELLIGENCES: THE THEORY IN PRACTICE. New York: Harper Collins.

Clarkson, Kenneth W., Miller, Roger LeRoy., Jentz, Gaylord A. & Cross, Frank B. (2009). BUSINESS LAW: TEXTS AND CASES. (11th ed.). Mason, Ohio: South-Western Cengage Learning.

Peters, B. Guy (2007). AMERICAN PUBLIC POLICY (7th ed.). Washington, DC: CQ Press.

Soccio, Douglas J. (2007). ARCHETYPES OF WISDOM (6th ed.). Belmont, CA: Thomson Higher Education.

United Staes Government. (2009). *U.S. Department of Transportation.* Retrieved July 25, 2009, from http://www.dot.gov/ethics/

Ruggiero, Vincent R. (2008). Thinking critically about ethical issues. Retrieved from https://ecampus.phoenix.edu/content/eBookLibrary2/content/DownloadFulfillment.aspx?url=http://ppdfapp.phoenix.edu/PpdfHandler/.fulfill?assetdataid=6edb0ce5-f3a3-4441-ad46-a7510a27feef&assetmetaid=bd36ed35-e2e9-443f-98cb-5abd2a6c328f&p=1.

Clarkson, Kenneth W., Miller, Roger LeRoy., Jentz, Gaylord A. & Cross, Frank B. (2009). *Business Law: Texts and Cases.* (11th ed.). Mason, Ohio: South-Western Cengage Learning.

Dry, M. (1985). *The constitutional thought of the anti-federalists.* American Political Science Association. Retrieved from http://www.apsanet.org/imgtest/ConstThoughtAntifederalists.pdf

Lewis, J. J. (2009). *Freedom quotes.* Retrieved from http://www.wisdomquotes.com/cat_freedom.html

Library of Congress. (1998). *Faith of Our Forefathers.* Retrieved from http://www.loc.gov/loc/lcib/9805/religion.html

Long, R. T. (1994). *The nature of law part II: the three functions of law* . Libertarian Nation Foundation . Retrieved from http://www.libertariannation.org/a/f1411.html#2.1

Mark, D. (2007). *Criticism of Constitution could have appeal.* Politico. Retrieved from http://www.politico.com/news/stories/1007/6413.html

Mount, S. (2010). *Constitutional topic: the federalists and the anti-federalists.* U.S. Constitution Online. Retrieved from http://www.usconstitution.net/consttop_faf.html

National Archives and Records Administration. (2010). *Three branches of government.* Retrieved from http://www.trumanlibrary.org/whistlestop/teacher_lessons/3branches/1.htm

Patterson, T.E. (2008). The American Democracy. Retrieved from https://ecampus.phoenix.edu/content/eBookLibrary2/content/eReader.aspx.

TheFreeDictionary. (2010). *New Deal.* Farlex, Inc. Retrieved from http://legal-dictionary.thefreedictionary.com/Roosevelt's+New+Deal

Mount, S. (2010). The Miranda warning. U.S. Constitution Online. Retrieved from http://www.usconstitution.net/miranda.html

Patterson, T. E. (2008). THE AMERICAN DEMOCRACY. Retrieved from https://ecampus.phoenix.edu/content/eBookLibrary2/content/TOC.aspx?assetdataid=9f81c77a-cd35-4dfa-aaa8-b4fa7a5304eb&assetmetaid=ab851e34-bc7f-45e4-94b5-5265f075185c

Clarkson, Kenneth W., Miller, Roger LeRoy., Jentz, Gaylord A. & Cross, Frank B. (2009). BUSINESS LAW: TEXTS AND CASES. (11th ed.). Mason, Ohio: South-Western Cengage Learning.

Patterson, T. E. (2008). THE AMERICAN DEMOCRACY. Retrieved from https://ecampus.phoenix.edu/content/eBookLibrary2/content/TOC.aspx?assetdataid=9f81c77a-cd35-4dfa-aaa8-b4fa7a5304eb&assetmetaid=ab851e34-bc7f-45e4-94b5-5265f075185c.

U.S. National Archives and Records Administration. (n.d.). *U.S. Electoral College.* Retrieved from http://www.archives.gov/federal-register/electoral-college/faq.html#process

U.S. Department of State . (2008). *Overview of national, state, and local governments in the United States.* Retrieved from http://www.america.gov/st/usg-english/2008/June/20080628195938ea ifas0.1860926.html

Cornell University Law School. (n.d.). First Amendment. Retrieved from http://topics.law.cornell.edu/wex/First_amendment

FindLaw. (2010). A history of the supreme court. Retrieved from http://supreme.lp.findlaw.com/supreme_court/supcthist.html

First Amendment Center. (2010). Freedom of Expression Topics. Retrieved from http://www.firstamendmentcenter.org/faclibrary/Library.aspx?section=expression

Greenberg, J. (2006). Supreme Court integration case will impact public schools. The Progressive. Retrieved from http://www.progressive.org/media_mpgreenberg113006

Mandell, Leonard B. (1998). U.S. Supreme Court - 1996 Term Cases of Significance to Local Practitioners. Retrieved from http://www.dcba.org/brief/febissue/1998/art10298.htm

New World Encyclopedia. (2009). Freedom of religion. Retrieved from http://www.newworldencyclopedia.org/entry/Freedom_of_religion

Supreme Court of the United States. (2010). A Brief overview of the supreme court. Retrieved from http://www.supremecourt.gov/about/briefoverview.aspx

TeacherVision. (2005). New York Times Co. v. United States. Pearson Education, Inc. Retrieved from http://www.teachervision.fen.com/us/supreme-court/cases/ar25.html

The History of the Supreme Court. (2010). Timeline: the court today. Retrieved from http://www.historyofsupremecourt.org/history/today/timeline.htm

The Religious Freedom Page. (n.d.). Widmar v. Vincent. Retrieved from http://religiousfreedom.lib.virginia.edu/court/widm_v_vinc.html

U.S. Supreme Court Media. (n.d.). Schenck v. United States. Retrieved from http://www.oyez.org/cases/1901-1939/1918/1918_437

Constitutional Rights Foundation. (2010). Young people and the internet. Retrieved from http://www.crf-usa.org/bill-of-rights-in-action/bria-15-4-a.html

FindLaw. (2009). Free speech lawsuits involving public schools. Retrieved from http://public.findlaw.com/education/student_rights_free_speech_lawsuits.html

Patterson, T. E. (2008). The American Democracy. Retrieved from https://ecampus.phoenix.edu/content/eBookLibrary2/content/eReader.aspx.

Internal Revenue Service. (2009). IRS Freedom of Information. Retrieved from http://www.irs.gov/foia/index.html

Comparative Studies in Society and History, (1959). Vol. 2, No. 1 pp. 49-66 (18 p). Cambridge University Press. Retrieved from:
http://www.jstor.org/stable/177546

Omohundro Institute of Early American History and Culture (1950). The William and Mary Quarterly Third Series, Vol. 7, No. 2 pp. 199-222 (24p). Retrieved from: http://www.jstor.org/stable/1917157

Price, S. (2001). Slavery's big victory. New York Times Upfront, 133(11), 23.

Van Camp, J. C. (2005). The first amendment. American Bar Association. Retrieved from http://www.csulb.edu/~jvancamp/freedom1.html

Find Law. (2009). *United States of America against Arthur Anderson, LLP.* Retrieved August 21, 2009, from http://news.findlaw.com/hdocs/docs/enron/usandersen030702ind.html

Flood, Mary. (2009). *The Case Against Arthur Anderson.* The Houston Chronicle. Retrieved August 21, 2009, from http://www.chron.com/disp/story.mpl/special/andersen/3157527.html

Kulzick, Raymond S. "Sarbanes-Oxley: effects on financial transparency." <u>SAM Advanced Management Journal</u> 69.1 (2004): 43(7). <u>General OneFile</u>. Gale Document Number:A113898253. Apollo Library. 18 Aug. 2009 <http://find.galegroup.com.ezproxy.apollolibrary.com/ips/start.do?prodId=IPS>.

PBS. (1998). *Bigger Than Enron*. Retrieved August 20, 2009, from http://www.pbs.org/wgbh/pages/frontline/shows/regulation/lessons/

Pickle, Hal B., & Abrahamson, Royce L. (1983). *Introduction to business* (5th ed.). Glenview, IL: Scott, Foresman and Company.

Securities and Exchange Commission. (2002). *Public Accountability Board.* Retrieved August 21, 2009, from http://www.sec.gov/news/press/2002-91.htm

Tuck. (2002). *Tuck School of Business at Dartmouth.* Retrieved August 19, 2009, from http://mba.tuck.dartmouth.edu/pdf/2001-1-0032.pdf

United States General Accounting Office. (2001). *Accounting Principles, Standards, and Requirements.* Retrieved August 21, 2009, from http://www.gao.gov/new.items/d02248g.pdf

Conner, Amy Johnson. "*American Bar Assn. survey shows tech budgets are scarce in small firms.*" Minnesota Lawyer (Oct 16, 2006): NA. General OneFile. Gale. Apollo Library. 29 Aug. 2009 <http://find.galegroup.com/itx/start.do?prodId=ITOF>. Gale Document Number:A152895927

Davis, Anthony E. and Jarvis, Peter R. "*Risk Management: Survival Tools for Law Firms*, 2d ed.(Brief article)(Book review)." Florida Bar Journal 81.11 (Dec 2007): 66(1). General OneFile. Gale. Apollo Library. 29 Aug. 2009 <http://find.galegroup.com/itx/start.do?prodId=ITOF>. Gale Document Number:A172636520

Euromoney Institutional Investor PLC. (1999). *American Bar Association Information Security Committee.*. Retrieved August 28, 2009, from www.abanet.org/scitech/ec/isc/home.html

Bateman, Thomas S., & Snell, Scott A. (2009). *Management: Leading and Collaborating In the Competitive World* (8th ed.). New York: McGraw-Hill/Irwin

Jamil Zainaldin "American Bar Association" *The Oxford Companion to American Law.* Kermit L. Hall, ed. Oxford University Press 2002. *Oxford Reference Online.* Oxford University Press   Apollo Group. 29 August 2009 http://www.oxfordreference.com/views/ENTRY.html?subview=Main&entry=t122.e0030

Bateman, Thomas S., & Snell, Scott A. (2009). *Management: Leading and Collaborating In the Competitive World* (8th ed.). New York: McGraw-Hill/Irwin

Belknap, Michal R. "American Judicature Society" *The Oxford Companion to American Law*. Kermit L. Hall, ed. Oxford University Press 2002. *Oxford Reference Online*. Oxford University Press Apollo Group. 1 September 2009 http://www.oxfordreference.com/views/ENTRY.html?subview=Main&entry=t122.e0031

Indiana Courts. (2006). *Supreme Court Jury Pool Project Receives National Award*. Retrieved September 4, 2009, from http://www.in.gov/judiciary/press/2006/0913.html

"Janet Reno to receive national award." <u>Palm Beach Daily Business Review</u> (Jan 20, 2009): NA. <u>General OneFile</u>. Gale. Apollo Library-Univ of Phoenix. 1 Sept. 2009 <http://find.galegroup.com/itx/start.do?prodId=ITOF>. Gale Document Number:A192564518

National Center for State Courts. (1998). *Judicial Selection and Retention.* Retrieved September 4, 2009, from http://www.ncsconline.org/WC/CourTopics/FAQs.asp?topic=JudSel

Wechsler, Mary. (2007). *Know Your Orgs.* Washington State Bar Association. Retrieved September 4, 2009, from http://wsba.org/media/publications/barnews/aug07-weschler.htm

Cronbach, Lee J. (1963). *Educational Psychology* (2nd ed.). New York: Harcourt, Brace & World, Inc..

Schroyens, Walter. (2005). Review of "Knowledge and Thought: An Introduction to Critical Thinking".. EXPERIMENTAL PSYCHOLOGY, 52 (2), 163-164. Retrieved September 13, 2009, from EBSCO host database. doi: 10.1027/1618-3169.52.2.163

Nielsen, Bayard D., Pickett, Cynthia L., & Simonton, Dean K. (2008). Conceptual versus experimental creativity: Which works best on convergent and divergent thinking tasks?. PSYCHOLOGY OF AESTHETICS, CREATIVITY, AND THE ARTS, 2(3), 131-138. Retrieved September 13, 2009, from EBSCO host database. doi: 10.1037/1931-3896.2.3.131.

Cronbach, Lee J. (1963). *Educational Psychology* (2nd ed.). New York: Harcourt, Brace & World, Inc..

Pascarella, Perry. "The secret of turning thinking into action." <u>Management Review</u> 86.n5 (May 1997): 38(2). <u>General OneFile</u>. Gale. Apollo Library-Univ of Phoenix. 11 Sept. 2009 <http://find.galegroup.com/itx/start.do?prodId=ITOF>. Gale Document Number:A19384249

http://www.das.state.or.us/DAS/EISPD/docs/Bus_Case_Template_V1.1.doc

Thoreau, H. D. (1995). *Walden; or life in the woods*. Toronto, Ontario: General Publishing Company.

Trevino, L. K., & Nelson, K. A. (2004). MANAGING BUSINESS ETHICS. Retrieved from https://ecampus.phoenix.edu/content/eBookLibrary2/content/DownloadFulfillment.aspx?url=http://ppdfapp.phoenix.edu/PpdfHandler/.fulfill?assetdataid=b4441d1d-f7b6-478c-b473-1ac64275d179&assetmetaid=96622e92-1322-4add-a1d4-50a5a239963d&p=1.

Clarkson, K., Miller, R.., Jentz, G., Cross, F. (2009). Business law: text and cases. Mason, OH: South-Western Cengage Learning.

Holy Bible: King James Version. (1989). Nashville: World Publishing.

Black, R. (1999). Black's law: A criminal defense lawyer reveals his defense strategies in four cliffhanger cases. New York, NY: Simon & Schuster.

Nelson, K., & Trevino, L. (2004). Managing business ethics: Straight talk about how to do it right (3rd ed.). New York: Wiley. https://ecampus.phoenix.edu/content/eBookLibrary2/content/DownloadList.aspx?assetMetaId=96622e92-1322-4add-a1d4-50a5a239963d&assetDataId=b545b568-814d-4105-a89f-fb69fdd56343

Trevino, L. K., & Nelson, K. A. (2004). *Managing business ethics: straight talk about how to do it right* (3rd ed.). Retrieved from https://ecampus.phoenix.edu/content/eBookLibrary2/content/DownloadList.aspx?assetMetaId=96622e92-1322-4add-a1d4-50a5a239963d&assetDataId=b545b568-814d-4105-a89f-fb69fdd56343

Nelson, K., & Trevino, L. (2004). Managing business ethics: Straight talk about how to do it right (3rd ed.). New York: Wiley. https://ecampus.phoenix.edu/content/eBookLibrary2/content/DownloadList.aspx?assetMetaId=96622e92-1322-4add-a1d4-50a5a239963d&assetDataId=b545b568-814d-4105-a89f-fb69fdd56343

Bateman, Thomas S., & Snell, Scott A. (2009). *Management: Leading and Collaborating In the Competitive World* (8th ed.). New York: McGraw-Hill/Irwin.

Clarkson, Kenneth W., Miller, Roger LeRoy., Jentz, Gaylord A. & Cross, Frank B. (2009). *Business Law: Texts and Cases.* (11th ed.). Mason, Ohio: South-Western Cengage Learning.

Nelson, K., & Trevino, L. (2004). Managing business ethics: Straight talk about how to do it right (3rd ed.). New York: Wiley. https://ecampus.phoenix.edu/content/eBookLibrary2/content/DownloadList.aspx?assetMetaId=96622e92-1322-4add-a1d4-50a5a239963d&assetDataId=b545b568-814d-4105-a89f-fb69fdd56343

Securitas AB. (n.d.). *Securitas in brief.* Retrieved from http://www.securitas.com/en/About-Securitas/Securitas-in-brief/

Nelson, K., & Trevino, L. (2004). Managing business ethics: Straight talk about how to do it right (3rd ed.). New York: Wiley. https://ecampus.phoenix.edu/content/eBookLibrary2/content/DownloadList.aspx?assetMetaId=96622e92-1322-4add-a1d4-50a5a239963d&assetDataId=b545b568-814d-4105-a89f-fb69fdd56343

Gray, J. R., & Thompson, P. M. (2004, June). Neurobiology of intelligence: science and ethics. Nature Reviews: Neuroscience, 5(1), 11.

Brill, A.A. (1995). *The basic writings of Sigmund Freud.* New York, NY: Random House, Inc.

Searle, J. (1984). *Minds, brains and science.* Cambridge , MA : Harvard University Press.

Terman, L. M., & Merrill, M. A. (1960). *Stanford-Binet intelligence scale.* Boston, MA: Houghton Mifflin Company.

Titus, H. H. (1970). *Living issues in philosophy* (5th ed.). New York, NY: D. Van Nostrand Company.

Clark, L. (2009, Fall). Understanding Intelligence. *Spectrum,* (1),

Soccio, D. J. (2007). Archetypes of wisdom: an introduction to philosophy (6th ed.). Belmont, CA: Thomson Higher Education.

Zeman, A. (2002). Consciousness: a user's guide. New Haven, CT: Yale University Press.

Gozzi Jr., R. (1997). Artificial intelligence- metaphor or oxymoron? ETC: A Review of General Semantics, 54(2), 219-224. Retrieved from http://search.ebscohost.com/login.aspx?direct=true&db=a9h&AN=9708074164&site=ehost-live

Schultz, A. C. (n.d.). The navy center for applied research in artificial intelligence. Department of the Navy . Retrieved from http://www.nrl.navy.mil/aic/index.php

VU University Amsterdam. (n.d.). Department of computer sciences. Retrieved from http://www.cs.vu.nl/en/research/artificial-intelligence/index.asp

Dürsteler, J. C. (2010). Syntactic knowledge and visual knowledge. InfoVis.net. Retrieved from http://www.infovis.net/printMag.php?num=146&lang=2

Frankl, Viktor E. (1984). MAN'S SEARCH FOR MEANING. New York, NY: Simon & Schuster.

Freeman, A., Mahoney, M. J., & Devito, P., Martin, D. (2004). COGNITION AND PSYCHOTHERAPY (2nd ed.). New York, NY: Springer.

Searle, J. (1984). *Minds, brains and science.* Cambridge , MA : Harvard University Press.

Zeman, A. (2002). *Consciousness a user's guide.* New Haven, CT: Yale University Press.

Schwartz, J. M., & Begley, S. (2002). The mind and the brain: neuroplasticity and the power of mental force. New York, NY: Harper Collins.

Frankl, Victor E. (1959). Man's search for meaning. New York, NY: Pocket Books: Simon & Schuster.

Gozzi Jr., R. (1997). Artificial intelligence- metaphor or oxymoron? ETC: A Review of General Semantics, 54(2), 219-224. Retrieved from http://search.ebscohost.com/login.aspx?direct=true&db=a9h&AN=9708074164&site=ehost-live

Searle, J. (1984). Minds, brains and science. Cambridge , MA : Harvard University Press.

Spotts, P. N. (1999). First tentative steps. Christian Science Monitor, 91(77), 1. Retrieved from http://search.ebscohost.com/login.aspx?direct=true&db=a9h&AN=1641322&site=ehost-live

Fredell, Eric. "AI's Impact Is Still Subtle But Is Growing." Government Computer News 5.1 (1986): 71. General OneFile. Web. 12 Jan. 2010. <http://find.galegroup.com.ezproxy.apollolibrary.com/gps/start.do?prodId=IPS&userGroupName=uphoenix>.

Newquist, Harvey P., III. "Random access AI." AI Expert Apr. 1994: 50+. General OneFile. Web. 12 Jan. 2010. <http://find.galegroup.com.ezproxy.apollolibrary.com/gps/start.do?prodId=IPS&userGroupName=uphoenix>. Gale Document Number:A15064103

Vasilash, Gary S. "The future of manufacturing: Mikio Kitano's dream of simpler machines & more humane organizations." Automotive Production Aug. 1996: 52+. General OneFile. Web. 12 Jan. 2010. <http://find.galegroup.com.ezproxy.apollolibrary.com/gps/start.do?prodId=IPS&userGroupName=uphoenix>.

Brown, N. (2007, Spring). Joseph Rosen, M.D.: Facing the future. Dartmouth Medicine, 31(3).

Nicholls, Linda. "Questions about our humanity cannot be answered simply." Anglican Journal June 2005: 5. General OneFile. Web. 14 Jan. 2010. <http://find.galegroup.com.ezproxy.apollolibrary.com/gps/start.do?prodId=IPS&userGroupName=uphoenix>. Gale Document Number:A133464210

"Why we need theologians." U.S. Catholic Sept. 1994: 16+. General OneFile. Web. 14 Jan. 2010. <http://find.galegroup.com.ezproxy.apollolibrary.com/gps/start.do?prodId=IPS&userGroupName=uphoenix>. Gale Document Number:A15786940

Chandler, T. (2002). Community science action guides. The Franklin Institute. Retrieved from http://fi.edu/guide/hughes/energyconservation.html

Fodor, J. A. (1981). The mind-body problem. Scientific American, 1.

Frank, K.. (2009, May 14). "The essential link between body and spirit". Jewish News,p. 25. Retrieved January 15, 2010, from Ethnic NewsWatch (ENW). (Document ID: 1733268341).

Hanlon, Michael. (2009, August 20). Are we on the brink of creating brink computer with a human brain? [Eire Region]. Daily Mail,20. Retrieved January 15, 2010, from ProQuest Newsstand. (Document ID: 1837703921).

Thomas, Kathy Q. (1997). University of Rochester. Rochester review. Retrieved from http://www.rochester.edu/pr/Review/V59N3/feature2.html

United States Department of Energy. (n.d.). Ask a scientist. Retrieved from http://www.newton.dep.anl.gov/askasci/phy00/phy00496.htm

Uzgalis, William L. (n.d.). The mind body problem. Oregon State University. Retrieved from http://oregonstate.edu/instruct/phl302/writing/mind-top.html

Epstein, R. G. (2000, Fall). Stories and Plays about Ethical and Social Implications of AI. ACM Intelligence Magazine, 11(3), 1.

Hibbard, B. (n.d.). *Open source AI*. University of Wisconsin-Madison. Retrieved from http://www.ssec.wisc.edu/~billh/g/hibbard_agi_workshop.pdf

Harris, P. (2010). • Rod Blagojevich guilty on just one count of 24 in corruption trial. The Guardian. Retrieved from http://www.guardian.co.uk/world/2010/aug/18/rod-blagojevich-guilty-one-count-corruption-trial

Soccio , D. J. (2007). *Archetypes of wisdom* . Belmont, CA: Thompson-Wadsworth.

Titus, H. H. (1970). *Living issues in philosophy* (5th ed.). New York, NY: D. Van Nostrand Company.

Winkler, K. P. (1996). An essay concerning human understanding. Indianapolis, IN: Hackett Publishing Company, Inc.

City of Tuscaloosa, AL. (2010). About. Retrieved from http://www.tuscaloosa.com/

uggiero, Vincent R. (2009). The art of thinking. a guide to critical and creative thought, ninth edition. Retrieved from https://ecampus.phoenix.edu/content/eBookLibrary2/content/eReader.aspx.

Ruggiero, Vincent R. (2009). The art of thinking. a guide to critical and creative thought, ninth edition. Retrieved from https://ecampus.phoenix.edu/content/eBookLibrary2/content/eReader.aspx.

Gentzkow, M., & Shapiro, J. M. (2008, Spring). Competition and truth in the market. Journal of Economic Perspectives, 22(2), 133–154.

Soccio, D. J. (2007). *Archetypes of wisdom*. Belmont, CA: Thompson-Wadsworth.

Alternative Radio. (2008). About Noam Chomsky. Retrieved from http://www.alternativeradio.org/speakers/CHON.shtml

ArticlesBase.com (2008). *Chomsky.* Retrieved from: http://www.articlesbase.com/languages-articles/chomsky-vs-skinner-624579.html

Boulder Integral, Inc. (2010). *Radical dialogues on enlightenment and the evolution of consciousness.* Retrieved from http://www.boulderintegral.org/tag/ken-wilber/

Crabtree, E. (1999). Noam Chomsky. Muskingum Department of Psychology. Retrieved from http://www.muskingum.edu/~psych/psycweb/history/chomsky.htm

Fodor, Jerry. "How the mind works: what we still don't know." Daedalus 135.3 (2006): 86+. General OneFile. Web. 12 Sept. 2010. Retrieved from: http://find.galegroup.com.ezproxy.apollolibrary.com/gps/infomark.do?&contentSet=IAC-Documents&type=retrieve&tabID=T002&prodId=IPS&docId=A149898429&source=gale&srcprod=ITOF&userGroupName=apollo&version=1.0 Gale Document Number:A149898429

Hemsell, R. (2002). Ken Wilber and Sri Aurobindo: a critical perspective. Infinity Foundation. Retrieved from http://www.infinityfoundation.com/mandala/i_es/i_es_hemse_wilber.htm

Macfarquhar, L. (2003) The devil's accountant. The New Yorker. New York: Mar 31, 2003. Vol. 79, Iss. 6; pg. 064. Retrieved from: http://www.scribd.com/doc/19019829/chomsky

Source Watch. (2010). Noam Avram Chomsky. Retrieved from http://www.sourcewatch.org/index.php?title=Noam_Chomsky

Young, J. E. (2002). A spectrum of consciousness for CEOS: A business application of Ken Wilber's spectrum of consciousness. International Journal of Organizational Analysis, 10(1), 30.

Arzola, G. (2000). Making a good team great. Across the Board, 37(9), 4. Retrieved from http://search.ebscohost.com/login.aspx?direct=true&db=bth&AN=3611294&site=bsi-live

Reeve, J. (2009). Understanding motivation and emotion. Retrieved from https://ecampus.phoenix.edu/content/eBookLibrary2/content/eReader.aspx.

Pojidaeff, Dimitri. (1995). The core principles of participative management. The Journal for Quality and Participation, 18(7), 44. Retrieved March 29, 2010, from ABI/INFORM Global. (Document ID: 8928679).

Chaplin, J.P. (1985). Dictionary of psychology (2nd ed.). New York, NY: Bantam Doubleday Dell.

Cherry, K. (n.d.). Social learning theory. About.com. Retrieved from http://psychology.about.com/od/developmentalpsychology/a/sociallearning.htm

Freeman, A., Pretzer, J., Fleming, B. & Simon, K., (2004). Clinical applications of cognitive therapy (2nd ed.). New York, NY: Kluwer Academic/Plenum.

Isom, M. D. (1998). The social learning theory. Florida State University. Retrieved from http://www.criminology.fsu.edu/crimtheory/bandura.htm

Laird, J. D., & Thompson, N. S. (1992). Psychology. Boston, MA: Houghton Mifflin.

learning-theories.com. (2008). Social learning theory (Bandura) . Retrieved from http://www.learning-theories.com/social-learning-theory-bandura.html

Morris, C.G. & Maisto, A.A. (1999). Psychology: an introduction (10th ed.). Upper Saddle River, NJ: Simon & Schuster.

LyricsMode. (2010). Chris Ledoux It Ain't The Years, It's The Miles lyrics. Retrieved from http://www.lyricsmode.com/lyrics/c/chris_ledoux/it_aint_the_years_its_the_miles.html

MindTools. (2010). Locke's goal setting theory. Retrieved from http://www.mindtools.com/pages/article/newHTE_87.htm

Reeve, J. (2009). Understanding motivation and emotion. Retrieved from https://ecampus.phoenix.edu/content/eBookLibrary2/content/eReader.aspx.

Automatic Data Processing, Inc. (2009). Strategies for manageing business during economic downturns and beyond. Retrieved from http://www.adp.com/tools-and-resources/case-studies-white-papers/~/media/White%20Papers/PEO/Strategies%20for%20Managing%20Businesses%20During%20Economic%20Downturns.ashx

Reeve, J. (2009). Understanding motivation and emotion. Retrieved from https://ecampus.phoenix.edu/content/eBookLibrary2/content/eReader.aspx.

Jex, S. M., & Britt, T. W. (2008). INTRODUCTION TO ORGANIZATIONAL PSYCHOLOGY. Retrieved from https://ecampus.phoenix.edu/content/eBookLibrary2/content/eReader.aspx.

Chaplin, J.P. (1985). Dictionary of psychology (2nd ed.). New York, NY: Bantam Doubleday Dell Publishing Group.

Jex, S. M., & Britt, T. W. (2008). Introduction to Organizational Psychology. Retrieved from https://ecampus.phoenix.edu/content/eBookLibrary2/content/eReader.aspx.

Foster, C. R. (1961). Psychology for life today. Chicago, IL: American Technical Society.

Morris, C. C., & Maisto, A. A. (1999). Psychology: an introduction (10th ed.). Upper Saddle River, NJ: Prentice Hall Inc..

Society for Industrial and Organizational Psychology. (2009). *What are SIOP and I-O psychologists?*. Retrieved from http://www.siop.org/Media/What.aspx

Warren, M. (2009). *Industrial organizational psychology.* Ohio University. Retrieved from http://www.ohio.edu/iopsychology/labs.cfm

Jex, S. M., & Britt, T. W. (2008). INTRODUCTION TO ORGANIZATIONAL PSYCHOLOGY. Retrieved from https://ecampus.phoenix.edu/content/eBookLibrary2/content/eReader.aspx

Clarkson, Kenneth W., Miller, Roger LeRoy., Jentz, Gaylord A. & Cross, Frank B. (2009). *Business Law: Texts and Cases.* (11th ed.). Mason, Ohio: South-Western Cengage Learning.

Jex, S. M., & Britt, T. W. (2008). Introduction to Organizational Psychology. Retrieved from https://ecampus.phoenix.edu/content/eBookLibrary2/content/eReader.aspx.

Kerns, C. D. (2009). Putting performance and happiness together in the workplace. Pepperdine University. Retrieved from http://gbr.pepperdine.edu/081/performance.html

Levitan, S. A., & Werneke, D. (1984). Worker participation and productivity change. Monthly Labor Review, (), 1-6. Retrieved from http://www.bls.gov/opub/mlr/1984/09/art5full.pdf

MacLane, C. N., & Walmsley, P. T. (2010). Reducing counterproductive work behavior through employee selection. Human Resource Management Review, 20(), 62–72. Retrieved from http://www.sciencedirect.com/science?_ob=MImg&_imagekey=B6W4J-4WGJKN0-1-3&_cdi=6544&_user=10&_pii=S1053482209000485&_orig=browse&_coverDate=03%2F31%2F2010&_sk=999799998&view=c&wchp=dGLbVlW-zSkzV&md5=663eed56cee2654c7a911e7ec6625289&ie=/sdarticle.pdf

University of Central Florida. (2009, Month). Job performance [PowerPoint slides]. Retrieved from http://www.bus.ucf.edu/mbardes/Chapter%202.pdf.

Jex, S. M., & Britt, T. W. (2008). INTRODUCTION TO ORGANIZATIONAL PSYCHOLOGY. Retrieved from https://ecampus.phoenix.edu/content/eBookLibrary2/content/eReader.aspx.

Cox, R. (2007). The transformational leadership report. Retrieved from http://www.transformationalleadership.net/products/TransformationalLeadershipReport.pdf

Cronbach, L. J., Hilgard, E. R., & Spalding, W. B. (1963). Educational psychology (2nd ed.). New York, NY: Harcourt, Brace & World, Inc.

Morris, C. G., & Maisto, A. A. (1999). Psychology: an introduction (10th ed.). Upper Saddle River, NJ: Prentice Hall.

University of Western Ontario. (n.d). Organizational theory and development [PowerPoint slides]. Retrieved from http://www.ssc.uwo.ca/psychology/undergraduate/psych266a/lectureslides/Lectures%202005/Psych%20266%20Org%20Theory.2005.pdf.

Engleberg, Isa N. & Wynn, Dianna R. (2010) Working in Groups: Communication Principles and Strategies, Allyn & Bacon: Pearson Education, Inc.

Engleberg, Isa N. & Wynn, Dianna R. (2010) Working in Groups: Communication Principles and Strategies, Allyn & Bacon: Pearson Education, Inc.

Larson, S. (2007). *What makes for an effective leader?*. Retrieved from http://www.managementhelp.org/mgmnt/leader.htm

Engleberg, Isa N. & Wynn, Dianna R. (2010) Working in Groups: Communication Principles and Strategies, Allyn & Bacon: Pearson Education, Inc.

Cooper, D. R., & Schindler, P. S. (2006). Business research methods. Retrieved from https://ecampus.phoenix.edu/content/eBookLibrary2/content/eReader.aspx.

Traub-Werner, D.. (2007). WHO SHOULD BECOME A PSYCHOANALYST? Canadian Psychoanalytic Society 50th Anniversary Congress Panel. Canadian Journal of Psychoanalysis, 15(2), 314-331. Retrieved October 10, 2010, from Research Library. (Document ID: 1415018071).

Ong, A. D. (2000). The impact of anonymity on responses to sensitive questions. University of Southern California. Retrieved from http://instructional1.calstatela.edu/dweiss/Psy542/Anonymity.pdf

Cooper, D. R., & Schindler, P. S. (2006). Business research methods. Retrieved from https://ecampus.phoenix.edu/content/eBookLibrary2/content/eReader.aspx.

Cooper, D. R., & Schindler, P. S. (2006). Business research methods. Retrieved from https://ecampus.phoenix.edu/content/eBookLibrary2/content/eReader.aspx.

Cooper, D. R., & Schindler, P. S. (2006). Business research methods. Retrieved from https://ecampus.phoenix.edu/content/eBookLibrary2/content/eReader.aspx.

Kottak, Conrad P., & Kozaitis, Kathryn A. (2003). ON BEING DIFFERENT: DIVERSITY AND MULTICULTURALISM IN THE NORTH AMERICAN MAINSTREAM, 2E. Retrieved from https://ecampus.phoenix.edu/content/eBookLibrary2/content/ereader.aspx?assetmetaid=d3dc4a6f-db70-4331-aede-ef2fb9918f8b&assetdataid=d9bf867f-3821-4437-8169-373462a91089.

Kottak, C. P., & Kozaitis, K. A. (2003). *On Being Different: Diversity and Multiculturalism in the North American Mainstream* (Second ed.). New York, New York: McGraw-Hill.

U.S. Equal Employment Opportunity Commission. (2009). *Equal pay act of 1963.* Retrieved October 13, 2009, from http://www.eeoc.gov/policy/epa.html

Haggerty, Barbara B. (correspondent). (2009, February 4). Faith Initiative Caught Between Church and State [Audio podcast]. *NPR.* Retrieved from http://www.npr.org/templates/story/story.php?storyId=100229826

Library of Congress. (1802). *Jefferson's Letter to the Danbury Baptists.* Retrieved from http://www.loc.gov/loc/lcib/9806/danpost.html

Department of Justice; Federal Bureau of Investigation. (2004). *Crime in the United States 2004.* Retrieved from http://www.fbi.gov/ucr/cius_04/offenses_reported/hate_crime/index.html

National Public Radio. (2009). *Congress Votes to Give Gays Hate Crime Protection.* Retrieved from http://www.npr.org/templates/story/story.php?storyId=114056942&ps=cprs

The Library of Congress. (2009). *Matthew Shepard Hate Crimes Prevention Act.* Retrieved from http://thomas.loc.gov/cgi-bin/query/D?c111:10:./temp/~c111QEXTRa::

Gullickson, Aaron. (2006). BLACK-WHITE INTERRACIAL MARRIAGE TRENDS, 1850-2000. Columbia University. Retrieved from http://paa2006.princeton.edu/download.aspx?submissionId=60719

Lang, Susan S. (2005). CHRONICLE ONLINE. Cornell University. Retrieved from http://www.news.cornell.edu/stories/Nov05/interracial.couples.ssl.html

Norris, Michele. (2007). LOVING DECISION: 40 YEARS OF LEGAL INTERRACIAL UNIONS . National Public Radio. Retrieved from http://www.npr.org/templates/story/story.php?storyId=10889047

Kottak, Conrad P., & Kozaitis, Kathryn A. (2003). ON BEING DIFFERENT: DIVERSITY AND MULTICULTURALISM IN THE NORTH AMERICAN MAINSTREAM (2nd ed.). New York, NY: The McGraw-Hill Companies.

United States Equal Employment Opportunity Commission. (2005). *EEOC Revises Guidelines on Timeliness on Filing Charges of Employment Discrimination.* Retrieved from http://www.eeoc.gov/press/7-21-05.html

University of Maine Cooperative Extension. (2004). *Group Works: Effective Communication* . Retrieved from http://www.umext.maine.edu/onlinepubs/PDFpubs/6103.pdf

Thomas, R. R., & Woodruff, M. I. (1999). *Building a house for diversity: The giraffe and the elephant.* Retrieved August 22, 2009, from http://www.psc.gov.yk.ca/pdf/building_a_house_of_diversity.pdf

Wark, Wendy W. (2008). HOW DIVERSE ORGANIZATIONS THRIVE. Inclusion Strategies. Retrieved from http://inclusionstrategies.net/index.htm

Ghosn, C. (n.d.). Diversity. Nissan. Retrieved from http://www.nissanusa.com/about/diversity/initiative.html

Green, K. A. (2009). Diversity in the Workplace. University of Florida. Retrieved from http://edis.ifas.ufl.edu/HR022

Schmit, J. (2004, May 7). Cracker Barrel customer says bias was 'flagrant'. *USA TODAY*. Retrieved from http://www.usatoday.com/money/companies/2004-05-07-cracker-barrel_x.htm

University of the Pacific. (2005). Cultural Diversity. Retrieved from http://www.pacific.edu/sis/mair/cultural-diversity.htm

U.S. Office of Personnel Management. (2000). Building and Maintaining a Diverse and High Quality Workforce. Retrieved from http://www.opm.gov/Diversity/diversity-3.htm

Dickinson, D. (2007). Combining people and technology: added value in security . Retrieved from http://facilities-manager.co.uk/security/combining-people-and-technology-added-value-in-security.html

Humbert, P.E. (2003). The Top 10 Ways to Add Extra Value. Retrieved from http://www.1001topwords.com/marketing1/sales/8180.php

Klein, M. (2004). PKWare launches new enterprise product line, adds new features to PKZip. Retrieved from http://wistechnology.com/articles/784/

Meadowcroft, B. (n.d.). The Impact of Information Technology on Work and Society. Retrieved from http://www.benmeadowcroft.com/reports/impact/

Motioncontrol.com - A Motion Control Marketing, Inc.. (2010). Newport corporation launches new products during the second quarter of 2004. Retrieved from http://www.motioncontrol.com/news/?id=553

NetCracker Technology Corp. (2005). NetCracker Technology announces new Customer Impact Analysis (CIA) Module. Retrieved from http://www.netcracker.com/en/news/press_releases/index.php?from4=9&id4=98

(2009). How New Technology Can Change the Customer's Decision Maker. Retrieved from http://technologymarketing.typepad.com/tmcleadersblog/2009/01/how-new-technology-can-change-the-customers-decision-maker.html

Regan, E. A., & O'Connor, B. N. (2002). End-user information systems: implementing individual and work group technologies, second edition . Retrieved from https://ecampus.phoenix.edu/content/eBookLibrary2/content/DownloadList.aspx?assetMetaId=9f9341ec-776c-4a2c-8e8c-422fc4e5f1fe&assetDataId=0c85207c-4579-445d-b2e5-278c996a3835 .

Richey, W. (2010). *Supreme Court: Does part of Patriot Act violate citizens' rights?*. Retrieved from http://www.csmonitor.com/USA/Justice/2010/0222/Supreme-Court-Does-part-of-Patriot-Act-violate-citizens-rights

Miller, R. (2008). Better tech support in 3 easy steps, part 3. ECT News Network, Inc. Retrieved from: http://www.ecommercetimes.com/story/63392.html?wlc=1280060010

Tadeo, A. (2009). How to build an effective team. Retrieved from: http://www.associatedcontent.com/article/1365632/how_to_build_an_effective_team.html?cat=55

Griggs, B. (2009, June 19). iPhone 3GS launch. Retrieved from http://www.cnn.com/2009/TECH/06/19/iphone.3gs.launch/index.html

Mehrmann, J. (n.d.) Implementing new technology. Retrieved from http://www.theallineed.com/computers/08052680.htm

(n.d.). Alignment of benchmarks and indicators. Retrieved from https://ims.ode.state.oh.us/ODE/IMS/ACS/Content/technology_standards_draft.pdf

(n.d.). Alignment of benchmarks and indicators. Retrieved from https://ims.ode.state.oh.us/ODE/IMS/ACS/Content/technology_standards_draft.pdf

(2010). Implementing new technology. Retrieved from http://www.whichwebdesigncompany.com/uk/articles/implementing-new-technology-1158

(2006). Understanding Basic Accounting. Finweek, 45. Retrieved from Business Source Complete database.

(n.d.). *American Bar Association.* Retrieved July 23, 2009, from https://www.abanet.org/home.html?ptc=global_home

Kilmann, Ralph H. (1989). *Managing Betond the Quick Fix.* San Francisco: Jossey-Bass.

Phillips, Jack J., & Bonner, Dede. (2000). *Leading Knowledge Management and Learning.* Alexandria, Virginia: ASTD.

Weinstein, Matt (1996). MANAGING TO HAVE FUN. New York: Fireside.

www.ingramcontent.com/pod-product-compliance
Lightning Source LLC
Chambersburg PA
CBHW051621170526
45167CB00001B/13